.....ask Helen

more

ABOUT QUILTING DESIGNS

Helen Squire

American Quilter's Society

P. O. Box 3290 • Paducah, KY 42002-3290

To the family and friends I name my designs after—
who inspire and encourage me always.
To those quilters who showed me their stitches
and asked me their questions. Thank you.

All photographs by MYRON MILLER

TABLE OF CONTENTS

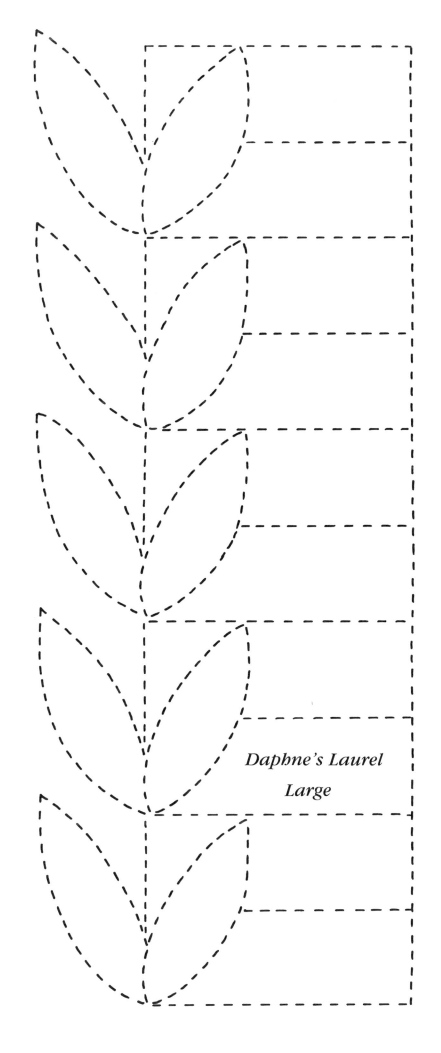

Daphne's Laurel

Large

DEAR HELEN, CAN YOU TELL ME—?

INTRODUCTION

This is a pattern book. It contains one hundred patterns. There are ten questions and answers placed throughout the book. They are typical of the reader's letters I receive and answer as columnist for **Lady's Circle Patchwork Quilts Magazine.**

These questions pertain to quilting and designing. Quilters want to know how to use plastic stencils or background grids. They ask if there are any rules to quilting, or what type of thread to use. They want to improve their stitches and miter borders. My answers include - "what to quilt, when to quilt it, and why."

In my first book, **Dear Helen, Can You Tell Me? . . . All About Quilting Designs,** the patterns are divided under six chapter headings FEATHERS * CABLES * CURVES * BORDERS * BLOCKS * GRIDS. In this book, **Ask Helen . . . More About Quilting Designs,** you will find another six headings

SASHING * SQUARES * CORNERS * KIDS * SHAPES and GRIDS II. For maximun use, take off the spiral binding and connect the pages into chapters with circle-rings, or loose-leaf binders that open and shut. The pattern pages can then be removed individually, copied, used and returned for later reference.

The pages are printed on one side only. This makes it easier to trace the pattern onto the quilt top when using a light-box or window. It also permits copying the design onto the blank side of the page. This automatically gives you the reverse, or flip-side of the pattern. This is especially helpful when planning borders and corners.

Precision piecing takes time and patiences. Applique is similar to painting - artistic and colorful. But quilting is special. The joining together of three layers makes a quilt.

The actual quilting stitch is only half of the art. Planning the quilting design to enhance the quilt is the other half. Begin by practicing Quilt Appreciation. In quilting, you have to learn what works and what doesn't. I refer to this as "raising ones quilting awareness level." Instead of trial and error, become self-taught. Go to quilt shows and exhibits. Read quilt magazines and books. Look again and again at pictures. Look closely. Start to recognize good quilting and what you like.

I hope you enjoy every "stitch" of this book.

Helen Squire

SMALLER SASHING STRIPS

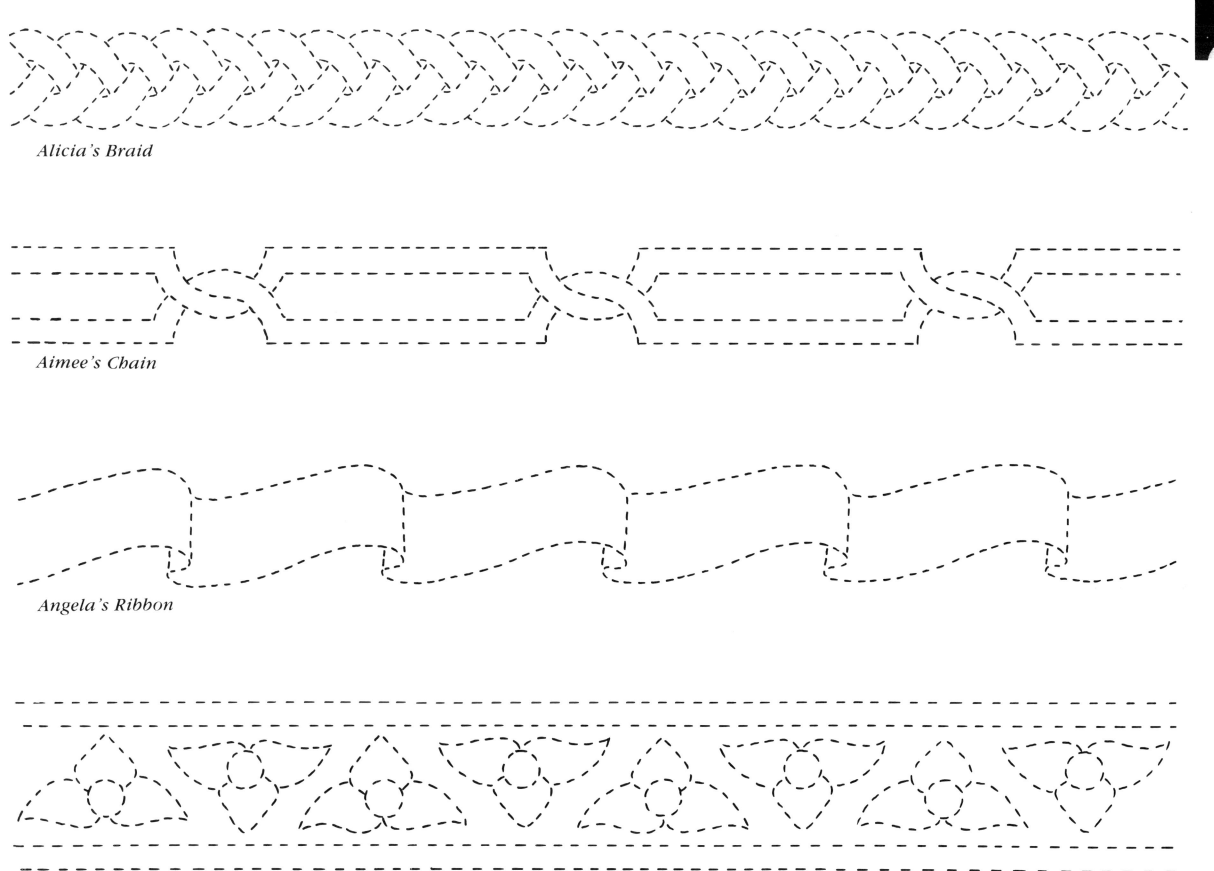

Alicia's Braid

Aimee's Chain

Angela's Ribbon

Alison's Petals

SMALL SASHING STRIPS

1 ½ " - 1 ¾ "

Betty's Twist & Twirl

Bab's Berries

Brenda's Lily

Bobbie's Blocks

Cathy's Quill

Carla's Conch

Caroline's Garden Lattice

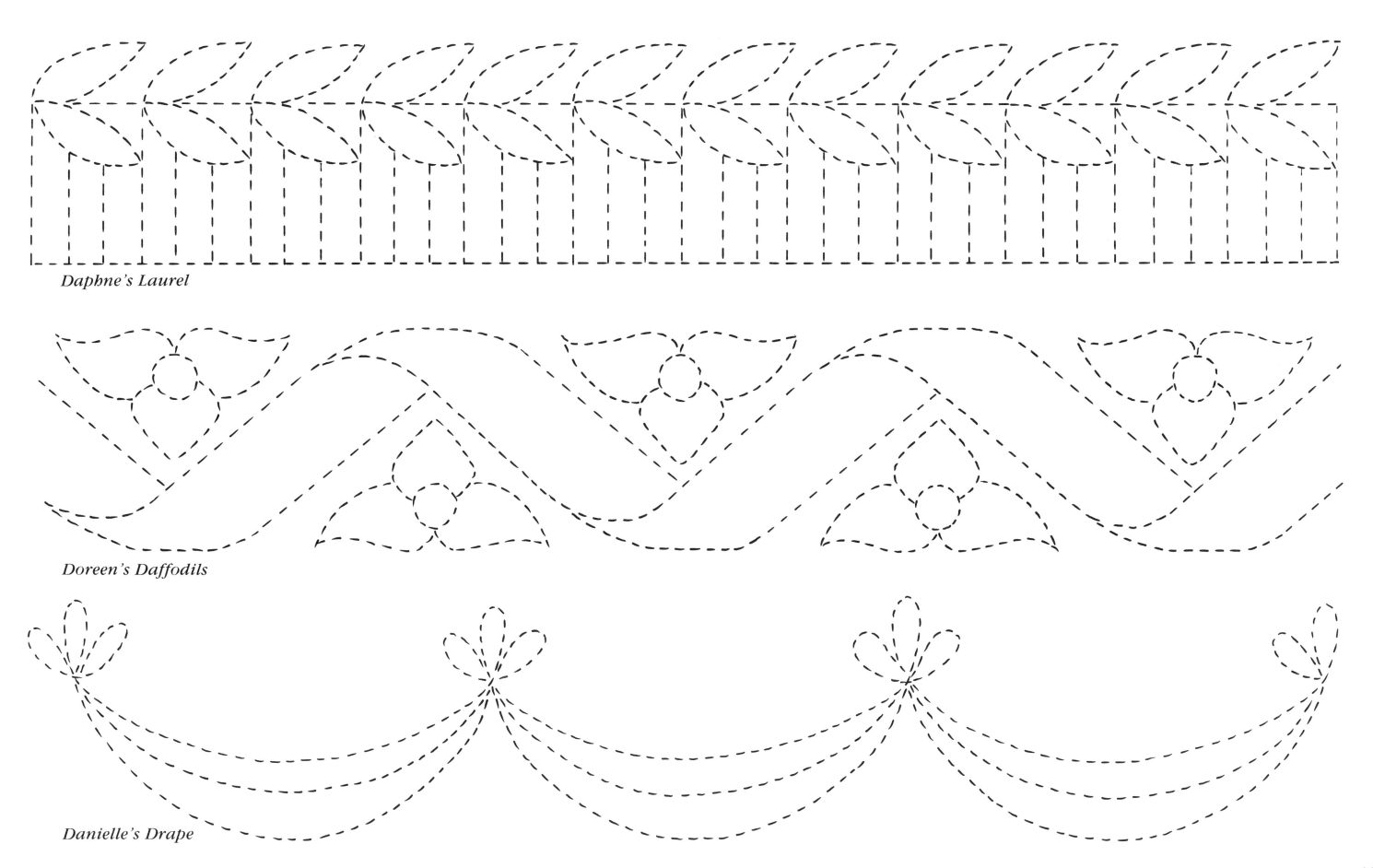

Daphne's Laurel

Doreen's Daffodils

Danielle's Drape

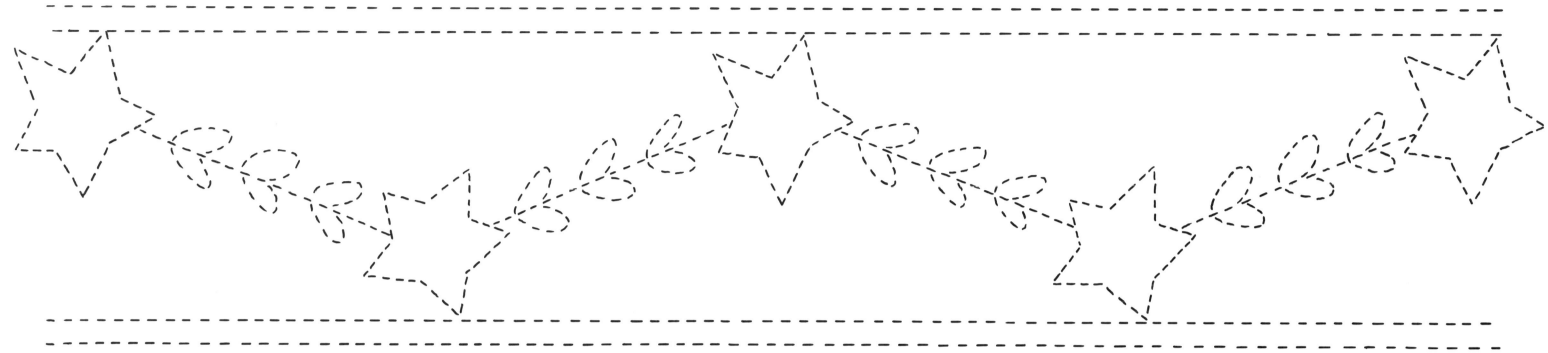

Elba's Star Flower

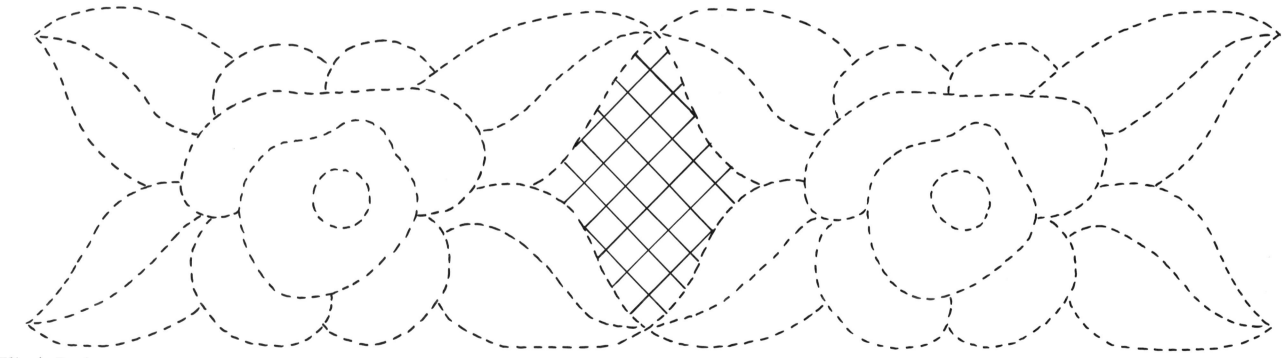

Elisa's Posies

The strip of fabric used to set patchwork blocks together is called sashing. If it is cut 3" wide, after sewing it will measure 2½" finished. How the seams are pressed (towards the block or under the sashing strips) will determine the size of the width to be quilted. "Outline" quilting is done ¼" away from the

seams. "In-the-ditch" quilting is done on the side with no seam allowances underneath. Select a pattern, then enlarge or reduce it to fit the final open area. Do not let the quilting design float in a space too big. Do not pick a size that means quilting along the extra thicknesses of seams.

Fran's Fence

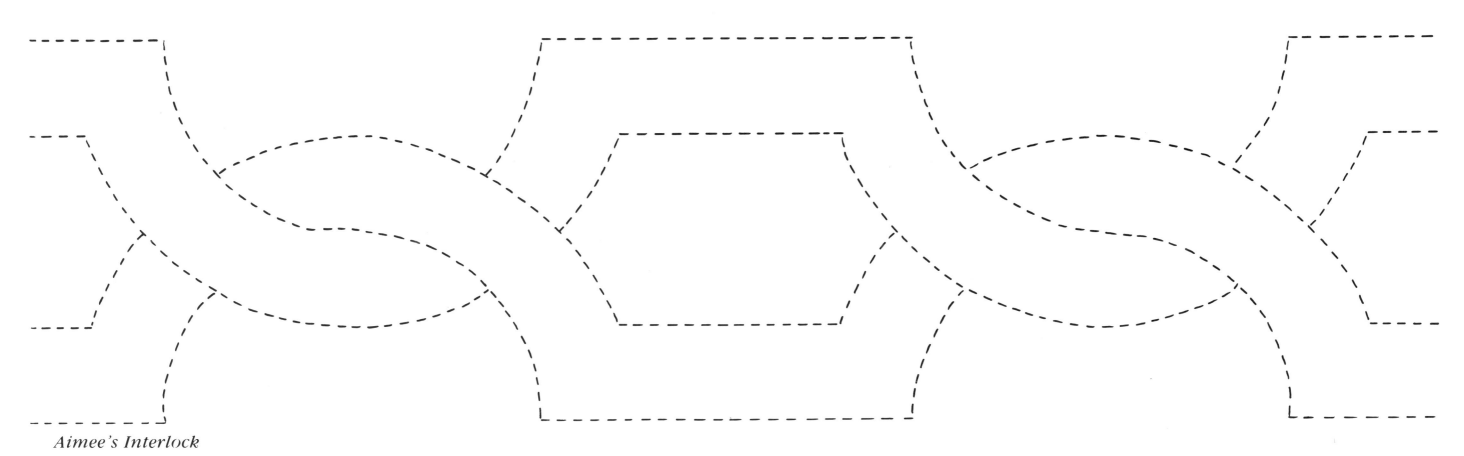

Aimee's Interlock

PUMPKIN SEED 2"

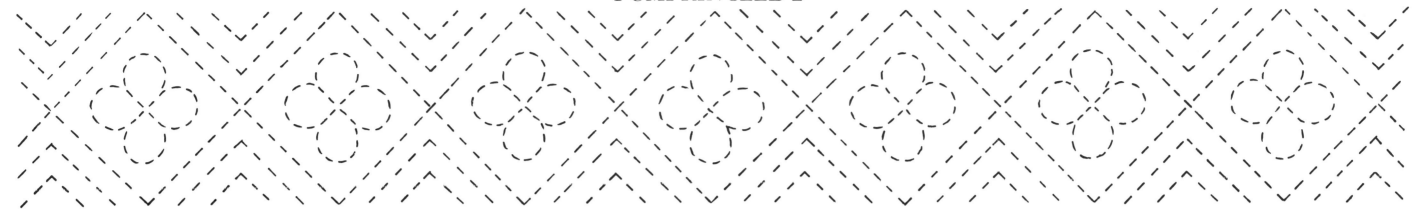

Ikuyo Saito made this pumpkin seed design for her traditional Amish Medallion wall quilt. Look what happens to the pattern as it is enlarged and reduced to fit various sashing widths. Notice the different ways possible to position the design. Try each way and decide which one you like before you start marking.

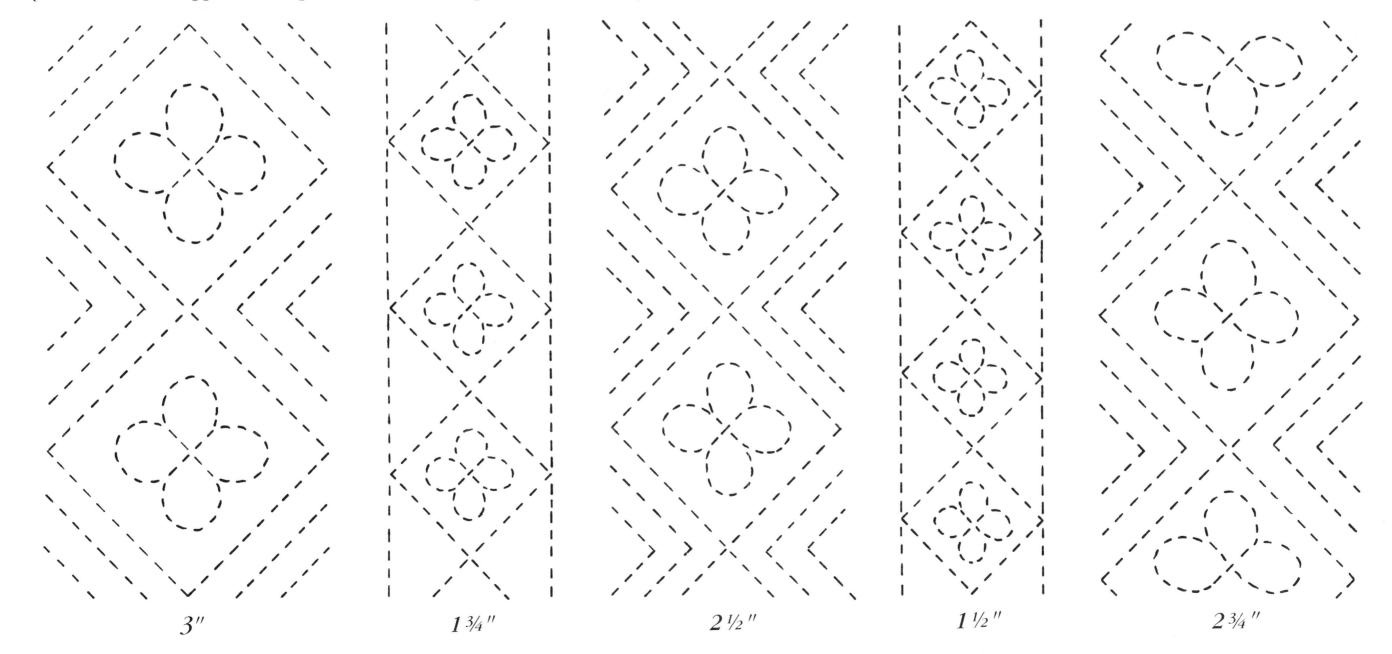

3"   1 ¾ "   2 ½ "   1 ½ "   2 ¾ "

 *"I hear so much about "mitered borders" and quilting designs that should "turn the corners." Would you please explain what this means?"*

 Quilting and borders should frame a quilt. Their purpose is to turn your eye back towards the main attraction.

Miters take more fabric and time to sew. They look nice but are really not necessary. For quilting however, it is nicer to plan your design *to look* as if it was mitered at the corners.

First make an imaginary miter by drawing a diagonal line from the edge of the quilt across the border width. Second, plan how many repeats of the quilting design fit around the quilt. You can use a silhouette of the shape, a stencil, or extra copies of the pattern.

I recommend using muslin, old white sheets, or large paper, one-fourth the size of the quilt, when designing. To plan the overall layout there are three places to begin: (1) the corners in to the center; (2) the centers out to the corner; (3) under each block (as in swags).

In all methods, copy the pattern up to the imaginary miter line. STOP. Flip or rotate the pattern and continue copying from the other side of the line. In this manner, any design can be made to turn a corner!

Alana's Lace Hanky

"As a beginner, I want to know what is considered good quilting. Is it taking small stitches like twelve to the inch?"

Good quilting is uniform stitches. The size of the stitch is equal to the space between. Beginners start with 3 to the inch, rapidly improve to 5, and average out around 7 stitches to the inch. This is measured by counting the stitches which appear *on the top*. Do not count back and top together!

To improve your stitch . . . practice! Use a grid of one-inch square. Take two or more sitches on your needle, pull the needle free, take more stitches, pull the needle free again. Now pull the needle *and thread* out. You will quilt faster and straighter. Count your stitches as you quilt.

Improvement is gradual. Figure 6 stitches x 3 inches = 18. Aim for another stitch and another, until you reach 21. This is now 7 stitches to the inch.

More important than small stitches, however, is *what* you quilt. Learn to analyze the flow of the design. Look for movement. Quilt cables and feathers in a flowing motion. Never quilt the outline of a flower and then go back and fill in the lines. Instead, quilt each petal as it would grow.

Pay attention to small details. Everytime you turn a corner you miss a stitch. Try quilting the horizontal lines first, then come in at the vertical lines from another direction. This gives you a stitch at both sides of the corner.

Look carefully throughout this book. I try to draw 5 stitches to the inch and in the best possible direction. I keep in mind . . . "If I can't draw it, you can't quilt it!"

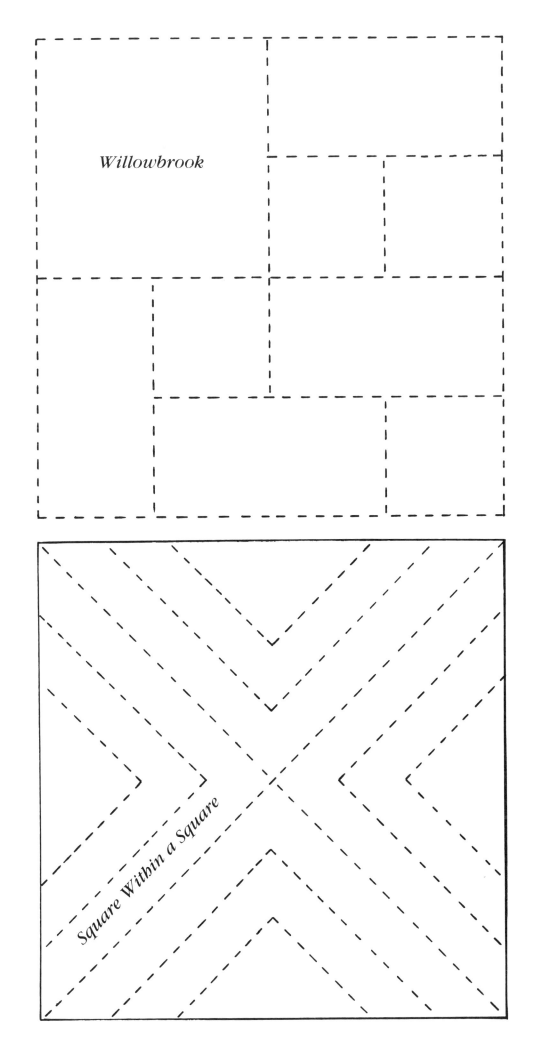

Willowbrook

Square Within a Square

Crosshatch

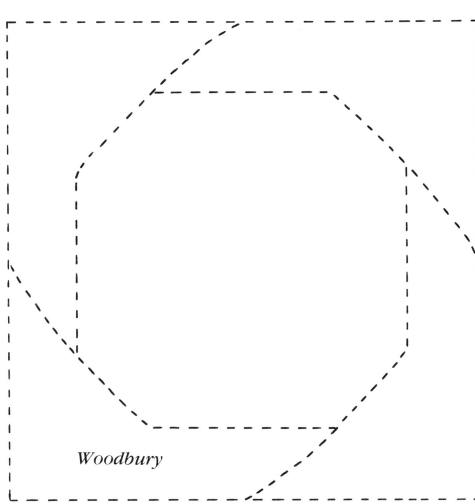

Woodbury

16

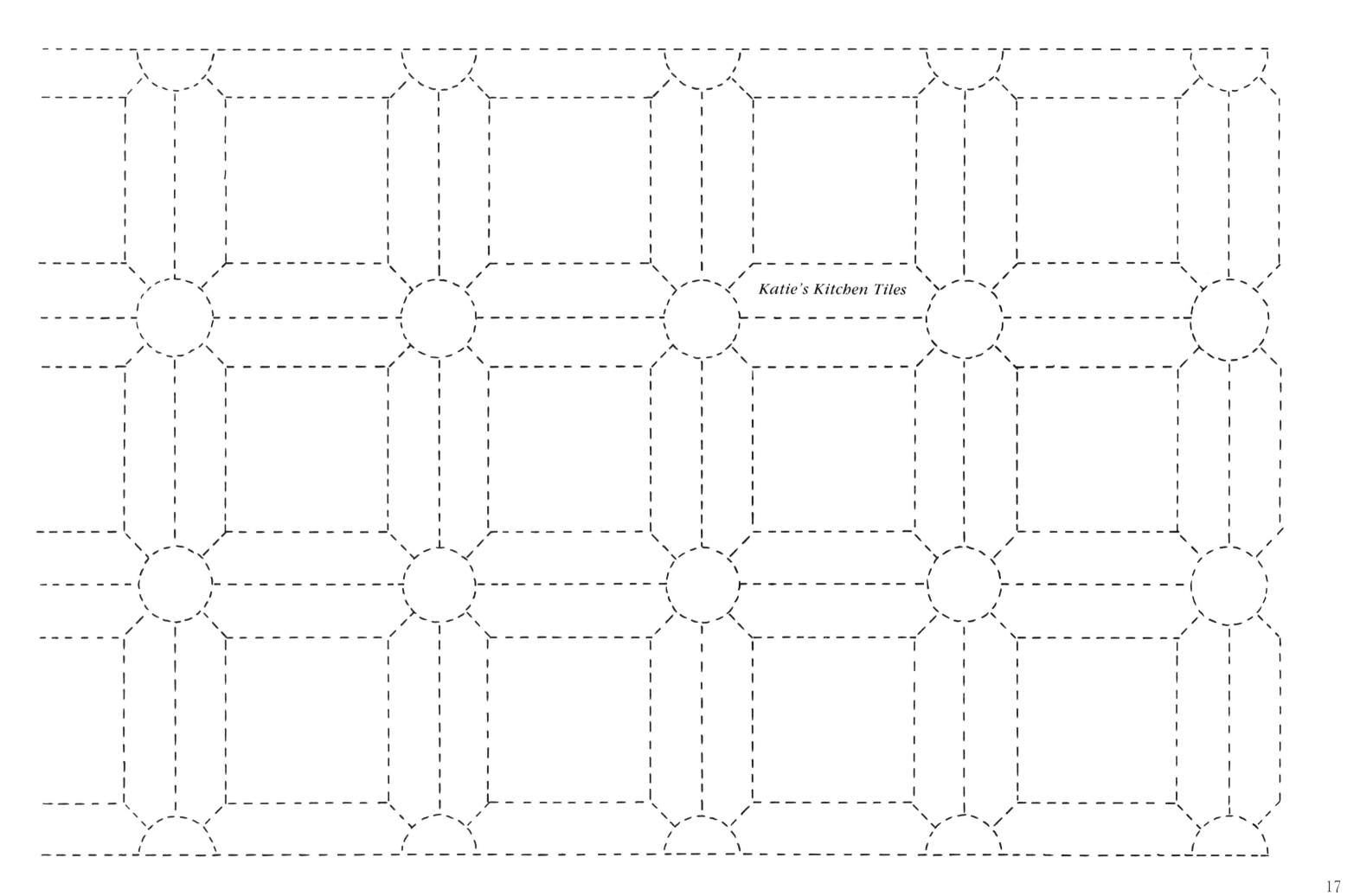

Katie's Kitchen Tiles

17

FLOWER MEDLEY QUILT

The best part of quilting—

The best part of any quilt is the quilting and whole cloth quilts are the most beautiful quilts of all!

In my book *DEAR HELEN, CAN YOU TELL ME . . . All About Quilting Designs,* I answered a request for pattern sources. From each of the other quilting and design books available I adapted a sample pattern. A MEDLEY OF FLOWER & BUTTERFLY DESIGNS I-IV was the result. This quilt uses those twenty-four, 5″ designs. I repeated some twice and used a large *Rose Wreath* applique pattern in the middle.

Rose colored satin is quilted with pink thread. This is sometimes called tone-on-tone quilting. A 1½″ folded ruffle finishes off this luxurious mini-quilt. *DESIGN V* adds three new butterflies and a perfect rose to the pattern series.

Costa Rica

Argentina

A MEDLEY OF FLOWER & BUTTERFLY DESIGNS V

Trinidad

Rosetta

18

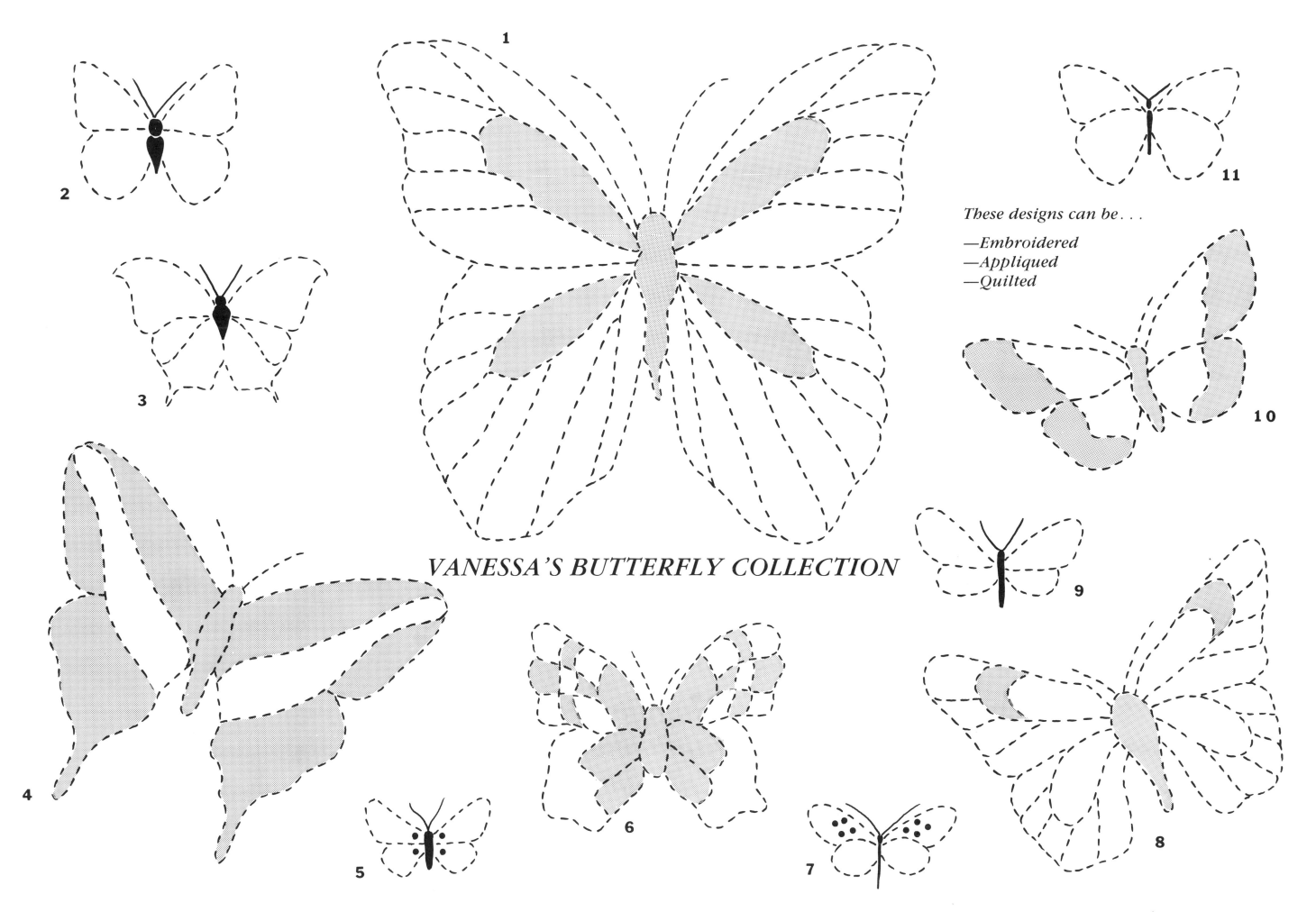

These designs can be . . .

—Embroidered
—Appliqued
—Quilted

VANESSA'S BUTTERFLY COLLECTION

 *"I want to make a quilt using different birds, hearts and flowers in the design. Any suggestions on where to begin?*

 If the design is hearts, flowers and birds, you need patterns with these elements. First look for compatible styles, then adapt them to fit your quilt. In this marvelous age of copy machines that reduce and enlarge by percentages, the hard part of combining different sized patterns is eliminated.

Look everywhere for ideas. The three patterns on the following pages come from sweatshirt and applique books as well as quilting books. The designers, *Virginia Robertson, Yvonne Amico* and *Shirley Thompson,* have graciously given permission for the inclusion of their patterns here, for your convenience, and so that I might use them to illustrate a point. I highly recommend their books.

The use of a circle with a background grid can unify or connect the smaller designs with the larger hearts. This prevents wide open spaces that would otherwise overpower the patterns.

My students use these patterns in the shadow applique method of sewing. Vivid colored fabrics are cut without seam allowances and glued lightly in place. *Quilter's Voile* fabric is placed on top and held in place with stitchery. The entire block is then batted-up and quilted.

Spring in the Air, Pennsylvania Dutch Design and *Love in Bloom* also work nicely for Trapunto. After quilting, slit the back and add extra, loose batting to stuff highlights of the designs. See my *Lovebirds* on page 23 for a visual comparison of both techniques.

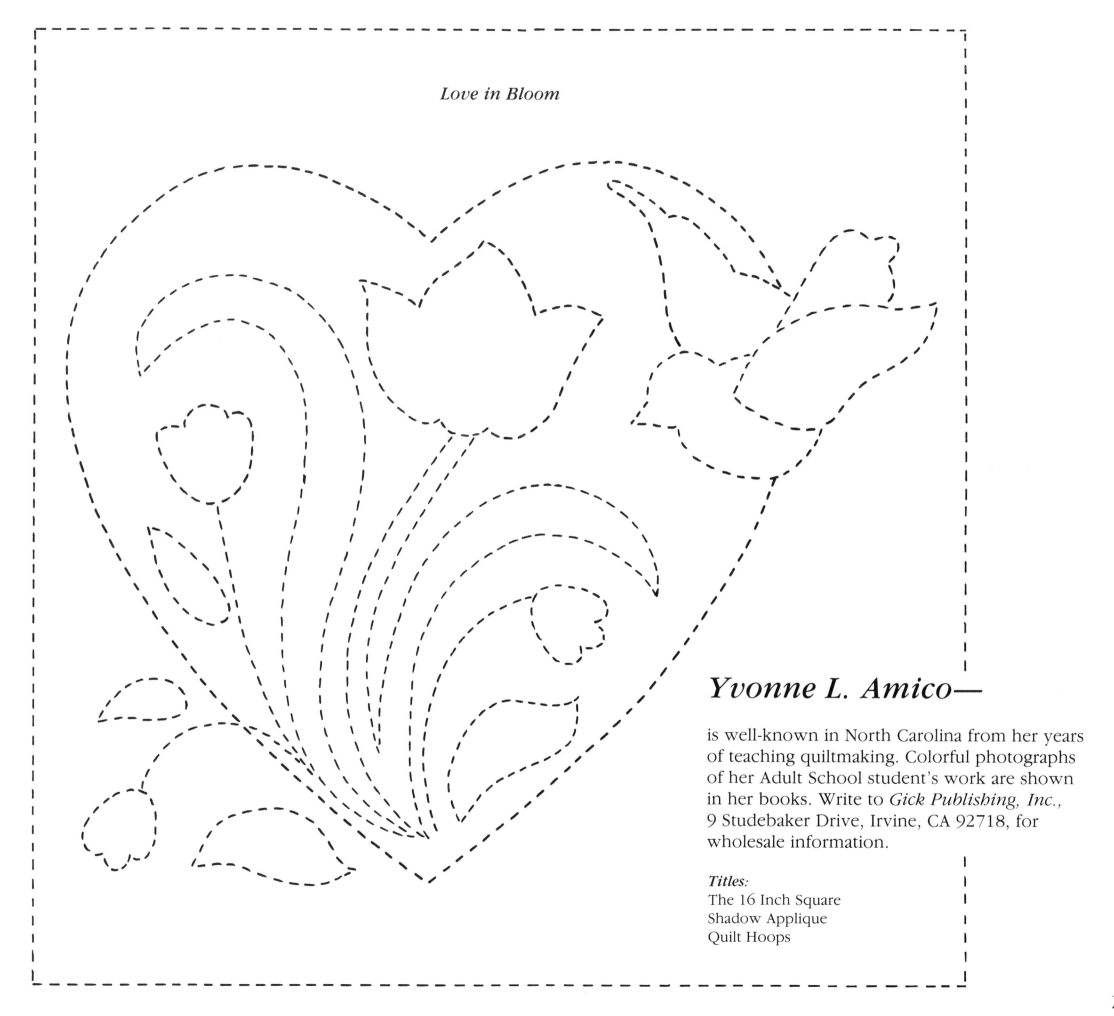

Love in Bloom

Yvonne L. Amico—

is well-known in North Carolina from her years of teaching quiltmaking. Colorful photographs of her Adult School student's work are shown in her books. Write to *Gick Publishing, Inc.,* 9 Studebaker Drive, Irvine, CA 92718, for wholesale information.

Titles:
The 16 Inch Square
Shadow Applique
Quilt Hoops

SHIRLEY THOMPSON'S

Pennsylvania Dutch Design

Design appears in her book:
It's Not a Quilt Until It's Quilted

Birds of a Different Feather

YVONNE L. AMICO'S

Love In Bloom

Design appears in her book:
Quilt Hoops

HELEN SQUIRE'S

Lovebirds

My design appeared in the magazine:
Creative Quilting, Grass Roots Publishers

VIRGINIA ROBERTSON'S

Spring In The Air

Design appears in her book:
Big Book of Sweatshirt Designs

Bird in a padded frame by Hisako Furutani.

Shirley Thompson—

hails from the State of Washington and specializes in quilting designs. Her huge collections of original and traditional patterns can be found in her many books on the subject. Order them directly from *Powell Publications,* Box 513, Edmonds, WA 98020. Also available at local quilt shops and from mail order firms.

Titles:
The Finishing Touch
It's Not a Quilt Until It's Quilted
Tried and True
Old-Time Quilting Designs

Pennsylvania Dutch Design

Lovebirds

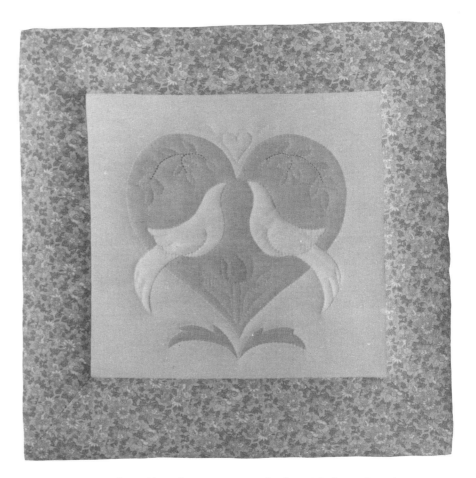

Framed quilt pictures made by Helen Squire.

23

Shadow applique picture made by Masako Kaseda.

Virginia Robertson—

is a fifth generation Kansas quilter. She has been teaching quilting and dollmaking since 1978. She publishes her own books of designs. They can be ordered from her shop, *The Osage County Quilt Factory* at 400 Walnut, Box 490, Overbrook, KS 66524, your local quilt shop, or from your favorite mail order source.

Titles:
Big Book of Quilting Patterns
Big Book of Applique Designs
Miniature Quilting Designs
Your First Quilt. . . And More
The Quilter's Colorbook

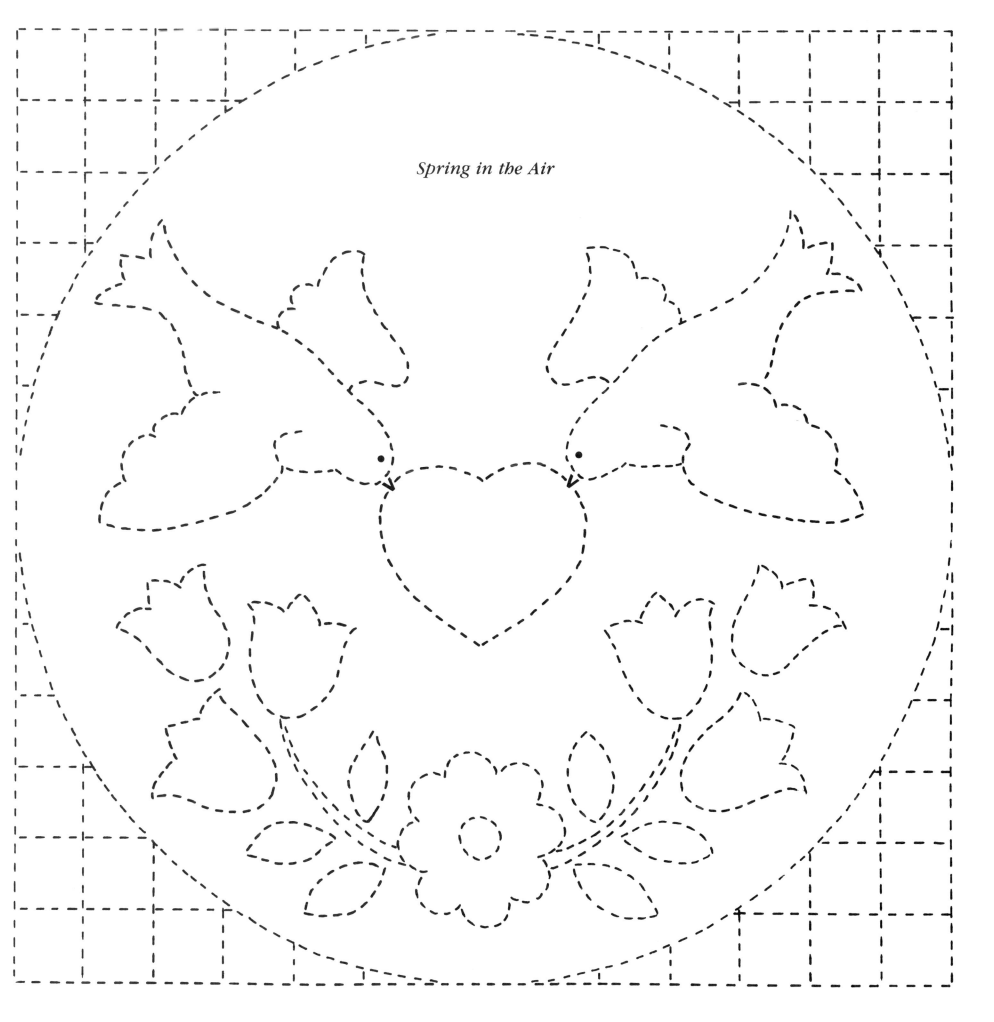

Spring in the Air

STARS AND STRIPES

A quilt to remember—

I teach many Japanese students in the metropolitan New York Area. Mrs. Tokiko Kato took lessons for three years. She began with pillows, piano covers, wall projects and small quilts. In the last year she made this quilt.

It was made to remember America. Simple, but bold, patchwork blocks are joined with rows and rows of borders. Everything sewn by hand. Mrs. Kato even borrowed an upright frame because she wanted it to be quilted "in the traditional way."

It is this attention to details; careful piecing, mitered border and adapting a quilting design to fit her specifications which makes it a cover quilt. This quilt can proudly be signed, "Made in America."

RICKEY 4½"

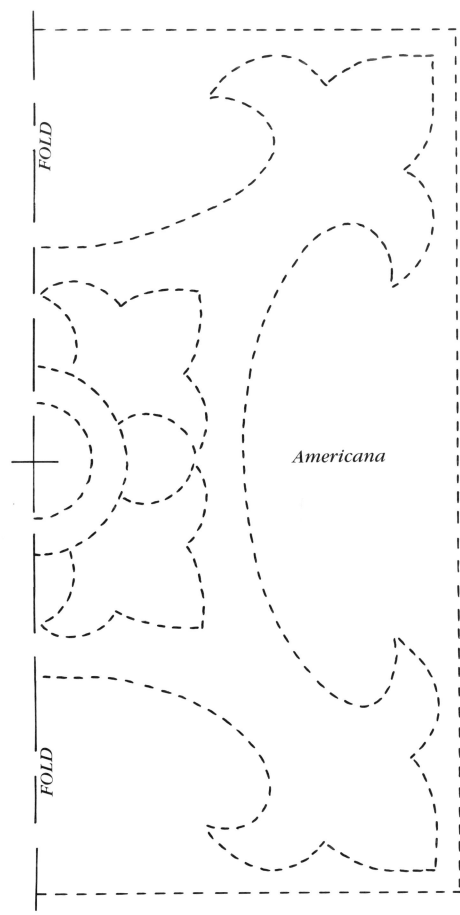

Americana

Fold plain paper. Copy pattern up to the fold, flip over and trace on other half. Use full pattern repeat to mark blocks.

Eight pointed star. Add ¼" seam allowances to pieces. The middle section is purposely made as a large square to give maximum quilting area. Quilt-in-the-ditch around triangles and squares. See the cover for close-up details.

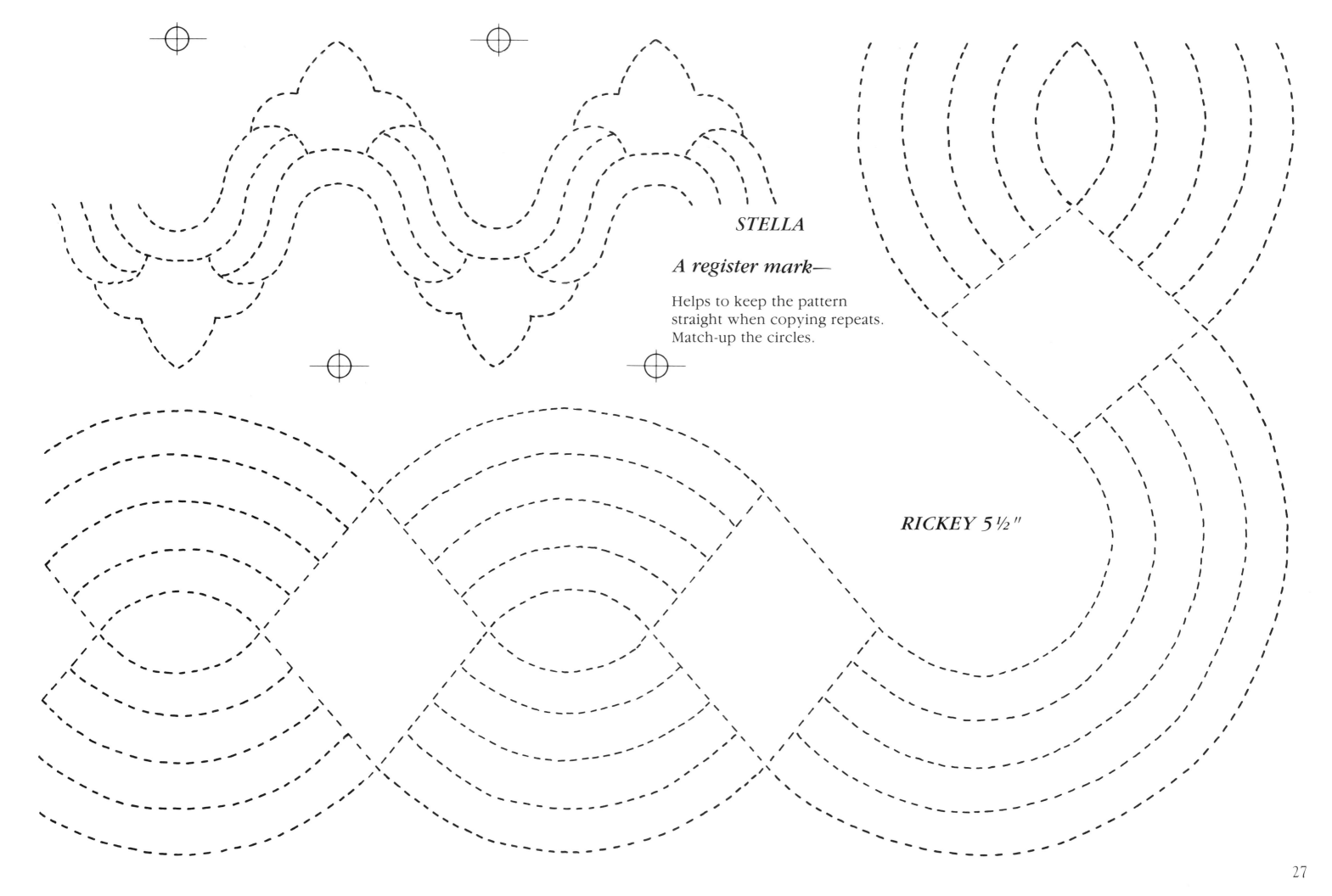

STELLA

A register mark—

Helps to keep the pattern
straight when copying repeats.
Match-up the circles.

RICKEY 5½"

 "Can you tell me if there are any rules to quilting? I want to try designing my own patterns but really don't know where to begin."

Here are some basic "rules": If the design is geometric then the quilting is flowing. If the design is flowing then the quilting is geometric.

Think of Amish quilts with their straight bars and center squares. The quilting is usually beautiful, moving feathers. Think of applique quilts. Most are flowing shapes with grids of vertical/diagonal lines.

Rule 1: *Curves and straight lines compliment each other. An area to be quilted should contain both.*

The more you quilt, the flatter it looks. The less you quilt, the fluffier it looks. With polyester batting, every 4 to 6 inches needs to be quilted. Cotton batting requires quilting every inch.

Rule 2: *Plan enough quilting to fill the space properly. Do not leave open areas.*

"Keep it simple. Less is best." Elaborate designs are impossbile to quilt and small details get lost. *Monica*, on the following page, is the simplified version of *Moroccan Maze.* The main element is the pointed arches. The repetion of this shape becomes interesting. It can echo a fabric motif or the name of a patch-work block.

Rule 3: *Create a design which pulls the entire quilt together.*

Phyllis' Philodendron

Wide band

Combination

Narrow band

SISTERS

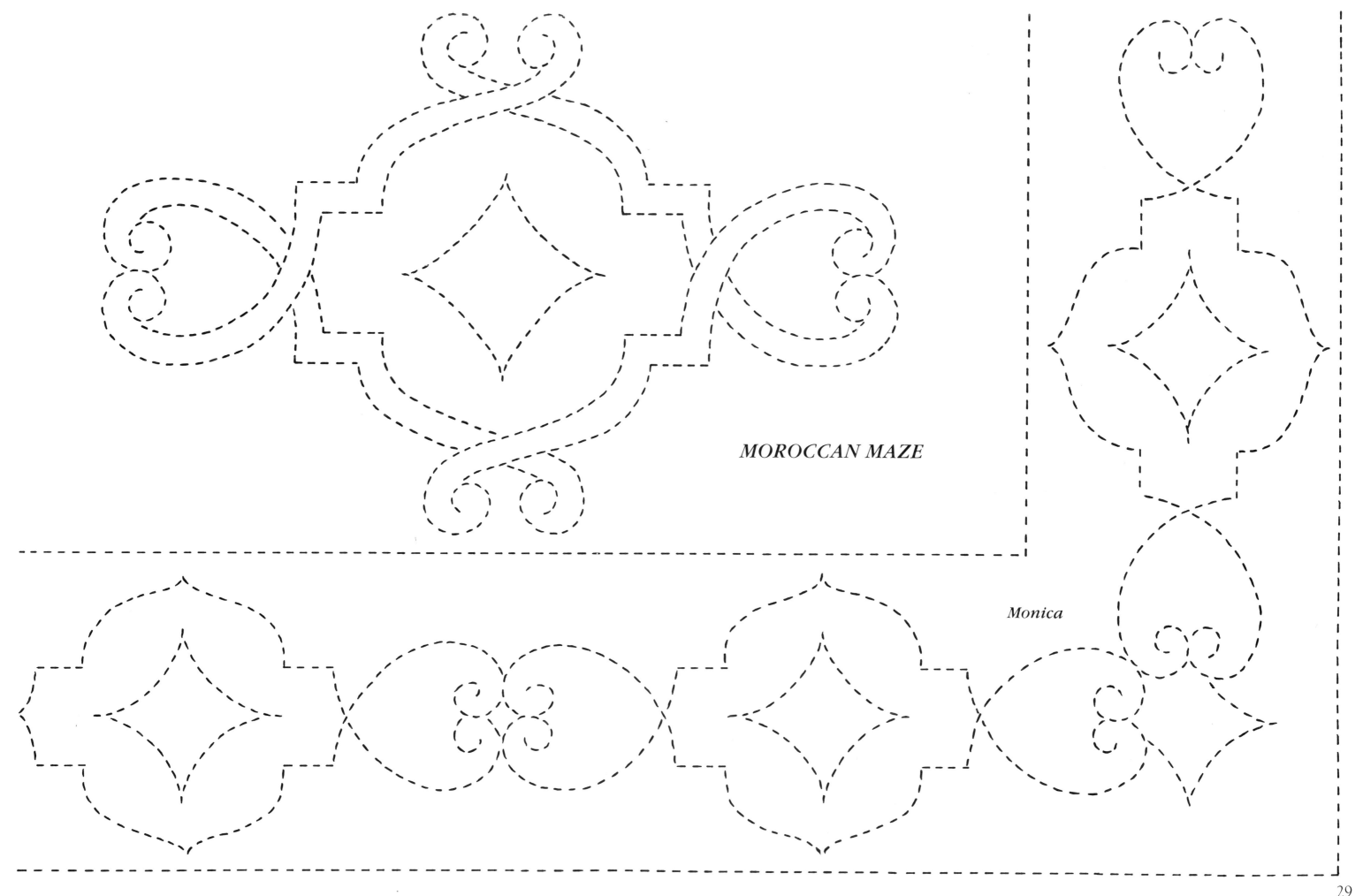

MOROCCAN MAZE

Monica

29

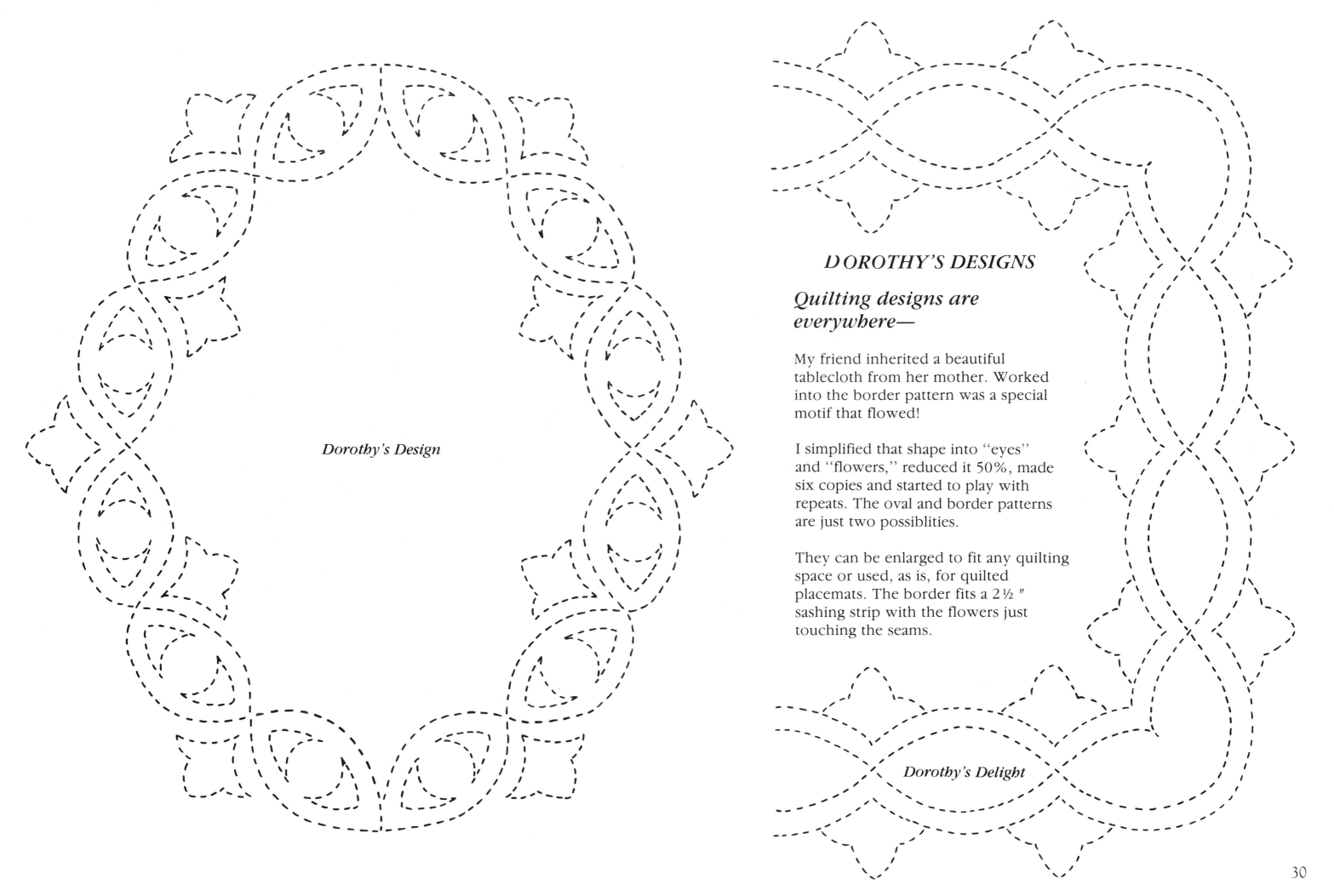

Dorothy's Design

DOROTHY'S DESIGNS

Quilting designs are everywhere—

My friend inherited a beautiful tablecloth from her mother. Worked into the border pattern was a special motif that flowed!

I simplified that shape into "eyes" and "flowers," reduced it 50%, made six copies and started to play with repeats. The oval and border patterns are just two possiblities.

They can be enlarged to fit any quilting space or used, as is, for quilted placemats. The border fits a 2 ½ ″ sashing strip with the flowers just touching the seams.

Dorothy's Delight

Gladys's Rose Garden

Koren's Companion Border

31

"Years ago I got an adorable panel of Mr. & Mrs. Mouse and now I want to use it in a quilt for my grandchild. Is it all right if the newer fabrics and colors don't match it?"

Make a theme quilt and no one will even notice! But it does require pre-planning to pull it all together.

Instead of the typical sampler quilt of many different designs and fabrics, I encourage my students to make quilts with three different sized blocks and a similar subject matter.

For example, to make a youth bed quilt (54" x 72"), you need a large center block, 30" square. To make it rectangular and to balance the math, sew a strip 3" x 30" to the left and right sides. Next attach the top and bottom rows. Piece six 12" blocks. Sew three on top and three on the bottom of the center section. Now make 24 - 9" blocks. Sew these around the outside of the quilt.

Here comes the fun part - picking the patterns. Appropriate choices are *Cats & Mice*, *Kitty Corner*, *Puss in the Corner* and *Puss in Boots*. Only pick one for the 12" blocks and one for the 9" blocks.

Mr. & Mrs. Mouse can be appliqued in the center of a huge *Puss in the Corner*. Any colors used in the pre-printed panel can be used in the blocks. Do not try to match them exactly. Pick tones and lighter and darker shades of the same colors.

For the quilting motif, try cats! Reclining, stretching, playful cats! Quilt-in-the-ditch around the blocks. The mice have to be outline quilted. Quilt any interesting details.

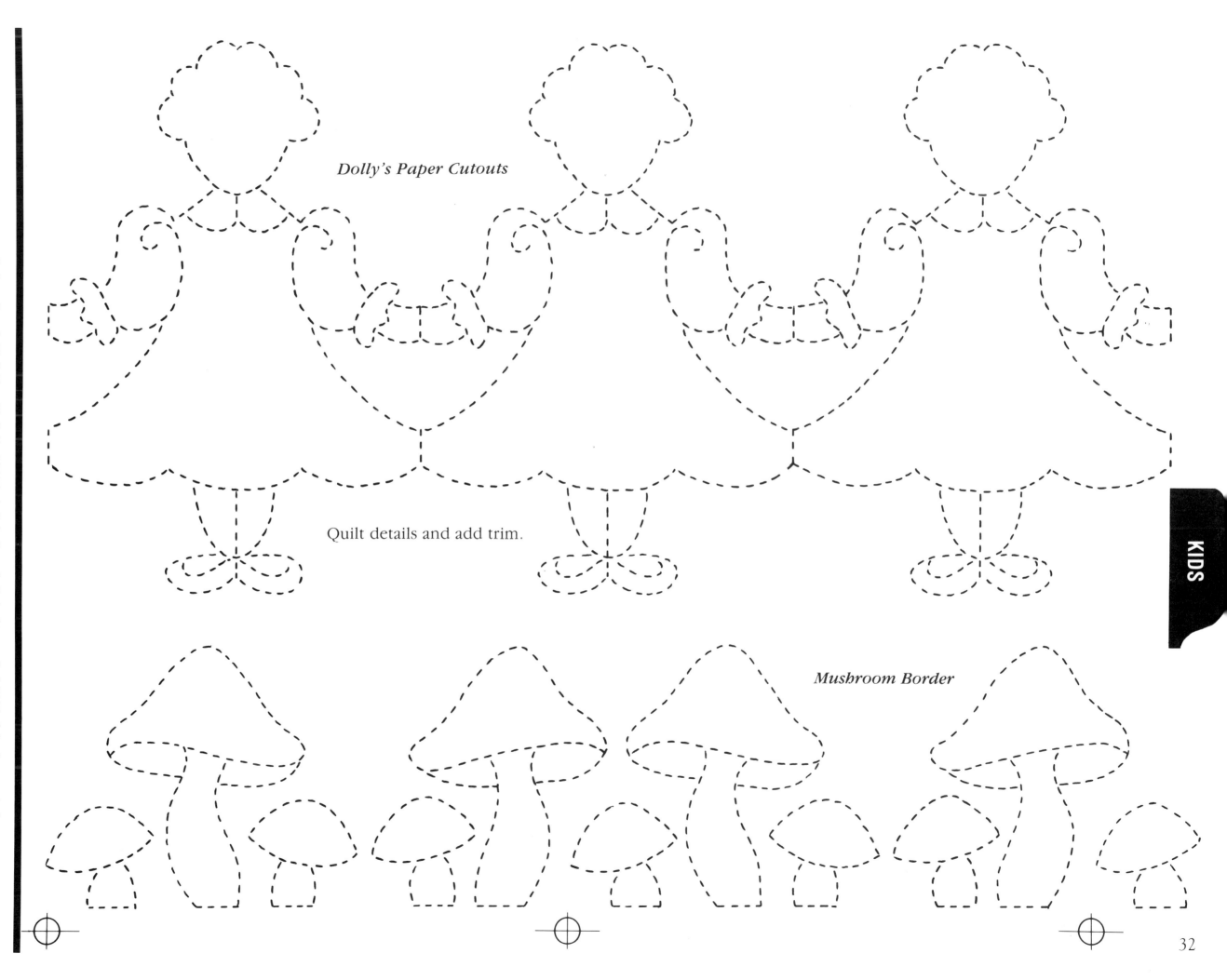

Dolly's Paper Cutouts

Quilt details and add trim.

Mushroom Border

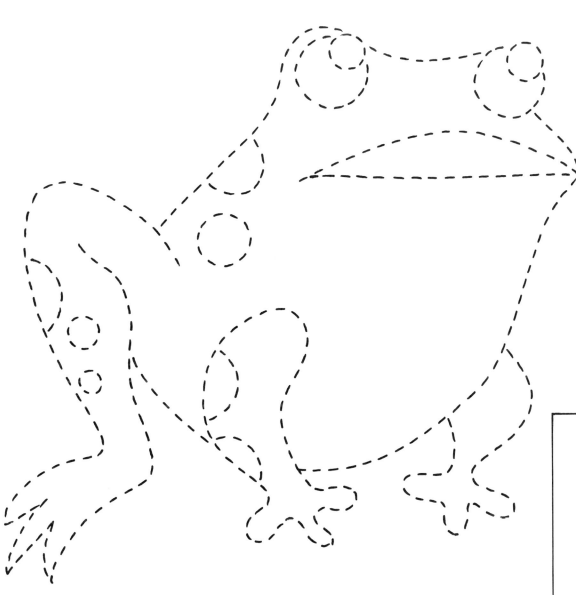

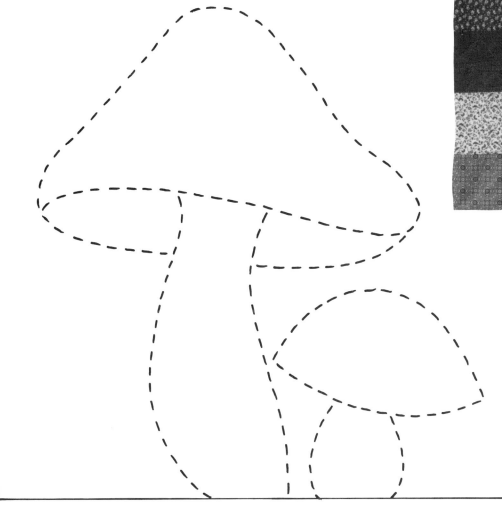

Mushroom Square

Printed animal panels—

Make perfect baby quilts. It is easy to design a co-ordinated quilt using pre-printed animal panels. Pick two or three main colors from the panel then use small, medium and large prints with solid fabrics to match. Also cut 6″ squares from the back of the panel to mix the actual printed fabric in with the patchwork.

The appliqued animal is outline quilted, after some details and trapunto were added first. The mushroom design is only quilted in the solid squares where it can be seen. In-the-ditch quilting is done everywhere else.

FROG QUILT

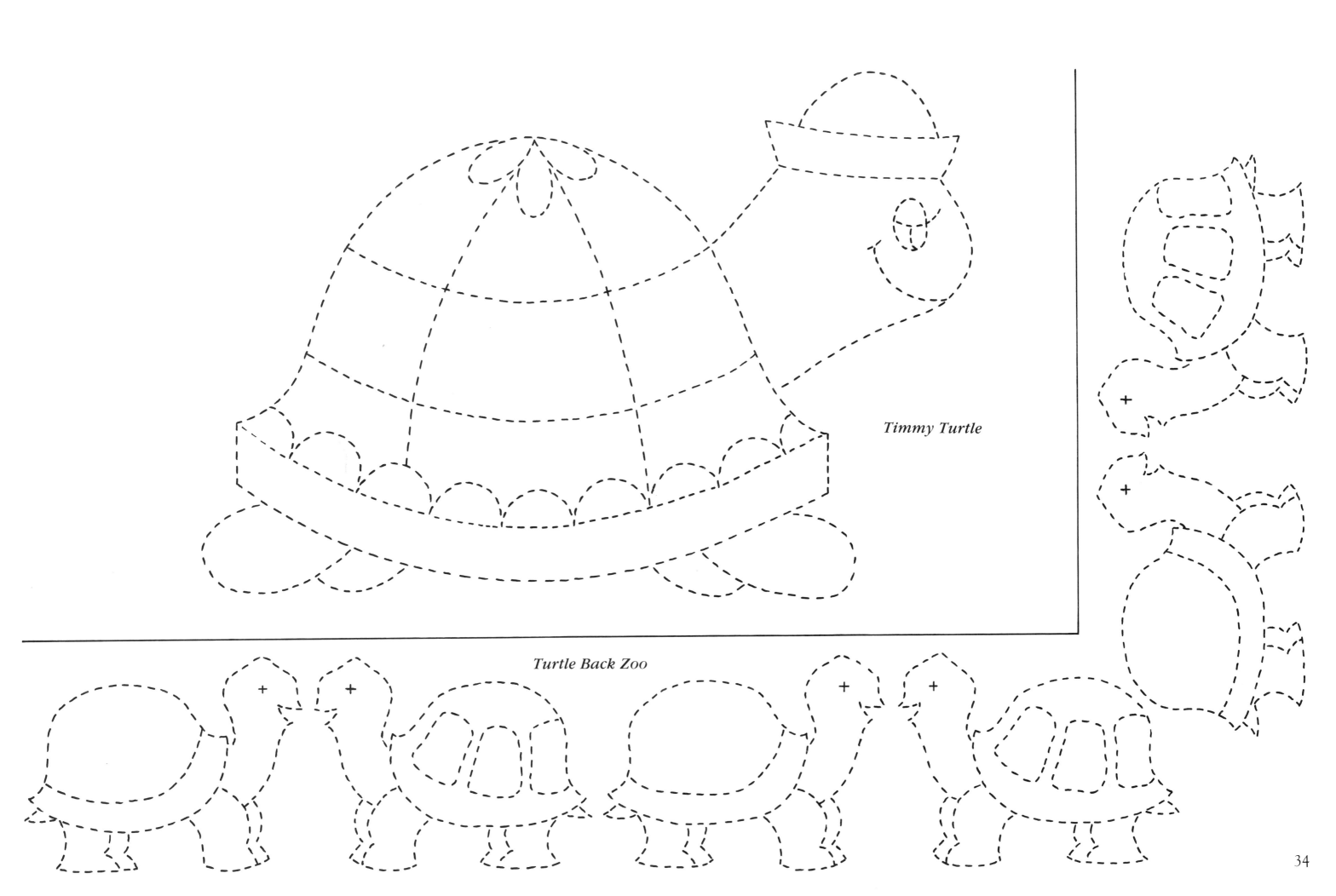

Timmy Turtle

Turtle Back Zoo

34

THREE BEARS QUILT

Let the quilting show—

Quilting is meant to be seen from all four sides. A young child will enjoy finding the quilted bears peering out in all directions. On this pre-printed panel, the only back piece big enough from which to cut out a patchwork square is the Daddy Bear. Notice his rear pocket on the bottom row.

After appliqueing in place, some areas were slit from behind, stuffed and sewn closed. The patchwork pieces were added, then the entire top was batted-up and quilted.

Bear's Face Square

Teddy Bear

35

TIGER QUILT

Lion Cub

Tiger Cub

36

 *"What do you know about using polyester thread for quilting? I have used some after treating it with parawax and it worked better than the regular quilting thread."*

 I know we are no longer limited to one source of quilting thread! More are being made and each has its own desirable characteristics: a high sheen, a large assortment of colors, a thicker denier or weight, different fiber contents - all cotton, all polyester or cotton-wrapped polyester.

White and the naturals (off-white, ecru, beige, etc.) account for over 75% of all thread sales.

Let me explain the most common brand names:

• *Tootal (Talon) American* is an English fabric and notion company who owns *American Thread*, which owns *Talon*, who in turns offers *Suisse* (pronounced sue-see) as one of their thread lines. These are all under the same banner but operate separately.

• *J.P. Coats* is the parent company and brand name of another English thread manufacturer. *Coats & Clark* is their United States sales agent.

• *Belding-Lily*, a.k.a. *Belding Corticilli* is owned by *Belding Heminway* and marketed by B. Blumenthal & Co.

• *Mettler Quilting Thread*, distributed by *Swiss-Metrosene*, is made of 100% cotton long fibers and comes in 32 colors. It sells well packaged or sold separately, but most quilters use it for applique and embroidery because it breaks too easily for quilting.

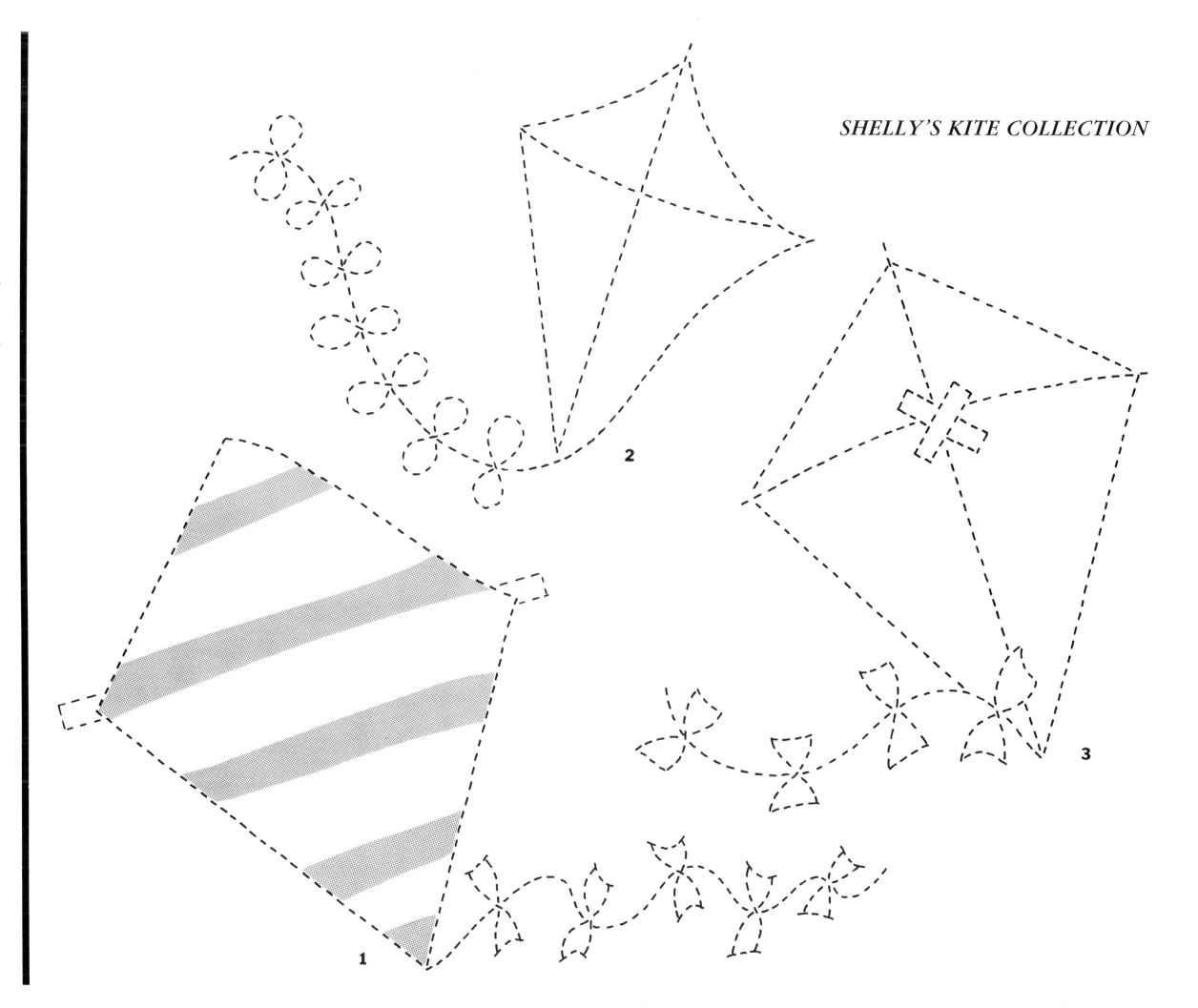

The actual technique for making a quilt with a pre-cut, slotted stencil is: (1) Position it over the area to be quilted. (2) Use an acceptable, pre-tested marker - a water erasable pen or chalk pencil. (3) Mark once through the slotted line with a steady sweep of the pen. (4) Remove and connect the shape by joining the missing links. This makes it easier to follow the design when quilting.

The benefits of this kind of stencil are: (a) You can mark before or after batting-up. (b) You can mark equally as well on light or dark colored fabrics. (c) A see-thru plastic permits accurate positioning.

The disadvantages are: (a) Cost. (b) Not always available in the size you need. (c) Limited use.

To make your own stencil: (1) Find the quilting design you like. (2) Trace it on a plastic sheet. These can be purchased at quilt shops or from mail-order firms. (3) Determine placement and length of slash. (4) Cut or burn away slots.

These firms specialize in pre-cut stencils. Send $2.00 for catalogs to:

THE STENCIL COMPANY
P.O. Box 1218
Williamsville, NY 14221

STENCIL AND STUFF
72 - 12th St. NW
Strasbury, OH 44680

OCEAN FANTASY

Whale

Sea Horse

Octopus

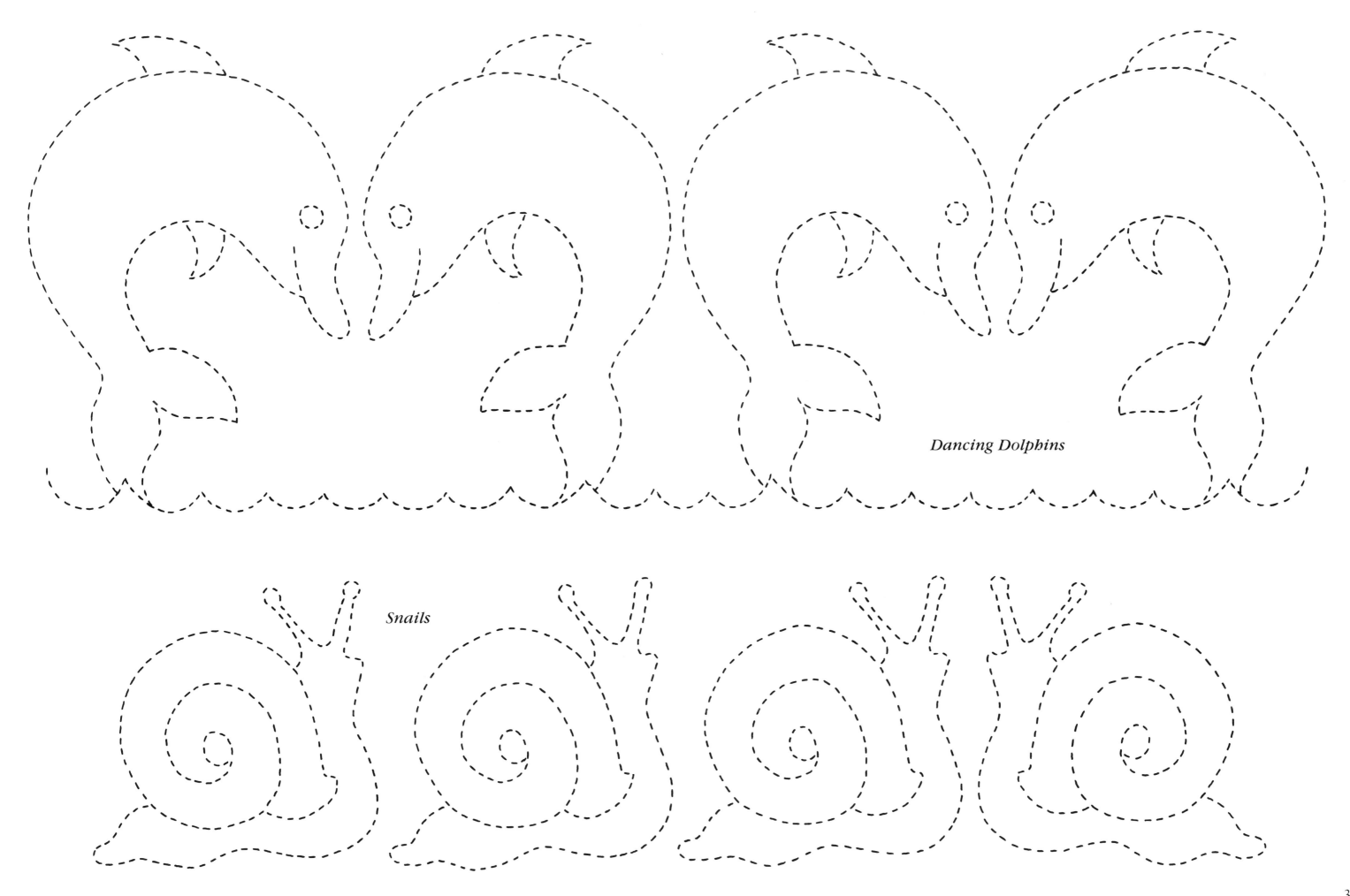

Dancing Dolphins

Snails

39

"I must be crazy! So many things that I see remind me of quilting. If I trace architectural carvings on buildings will they make good quilting designs or are they too fancy to use?"

Tracing scrolls, etc., from buildings is a wonderful source of designs. Bas-relief carvings have a dimensional effect needed for quilting. Look for the repeat (where and how it connects). Try to copy two. Sketch those you cannot reach.

Another way is using the excellent research books in the DOVER *Pictorial Archive* SERIES. From Byzantine (Aimee) to Grecian (Bobbie), I find unlimited inspiration in these books. Two favorites from Dover Publications, Inc. are:

• *ORNAMENTAL BORDERS, SCROLLS AND CARTOUCHES in Historic Decorative Styles* by the Syracuse Ornamental Company.

• *AMERICAN FOLK ART DESIGNS AND MOTIFS for Artists and Craftspeople* by Joseph D'Addetta.

No design is too fancy to use. Remember to simplify the design. Compare Figure 1 (below) to *Georgette* and *Georgina.*

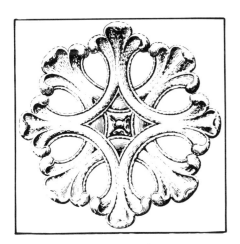

SCROLLS: English Renaissance

Georgette

Georgina

Entwined

Embossed

Feathered

HEARTS GALORE

First consider the placement of any all-over quilting design. Make a quilt worksheet of the size, blocks and borders. Graph paper with see-thru tracing paper taped over the quilt layout gives you the ability to "play with" the placement of where to begin quilting the open areas. The lines or shapes can then be adjusted to fit a given space before you quilt.

The diamonds should be *balanced* or *corner-to-corner* (Fig. 1 - Fig. 2) instead of ending in a haphazard manner. Quilting lines do not have to be mathmetically precise but they do have to be visually pleasing, as well as, structually sound.

Using the graceful clamshell has its own requirements. When this shape is used as a background, the placement of the first row must be considered.

On separate paper, have four or five rows of clamshell drawn. This is what is referred to as a grid. Slip it under the fabric and position it so that the first row of clamshells starts and ends with a half-shell (Fig. 3) or a full-shell (Fig. 4). Trace, move the grid, continue copying. The sides of the quilt should match, but not necessarily the top and bottom rows.

If the fabric is too dark to see through and trace, refer to your grid for placement only. Use dressmaker's chalk and a ruler or masking tape for marking grid lines.

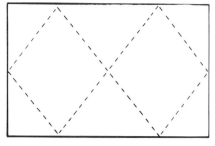

Figure 1
BALANCED

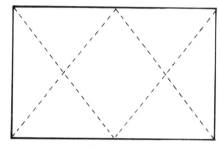

Figure 2
CORNER-TO-CORNER

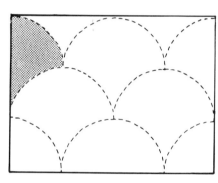

Figure 3
HALF CLAMSHELL

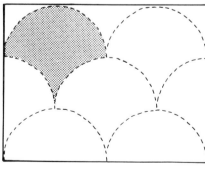

Figure 4
FULL CLAMSHELL

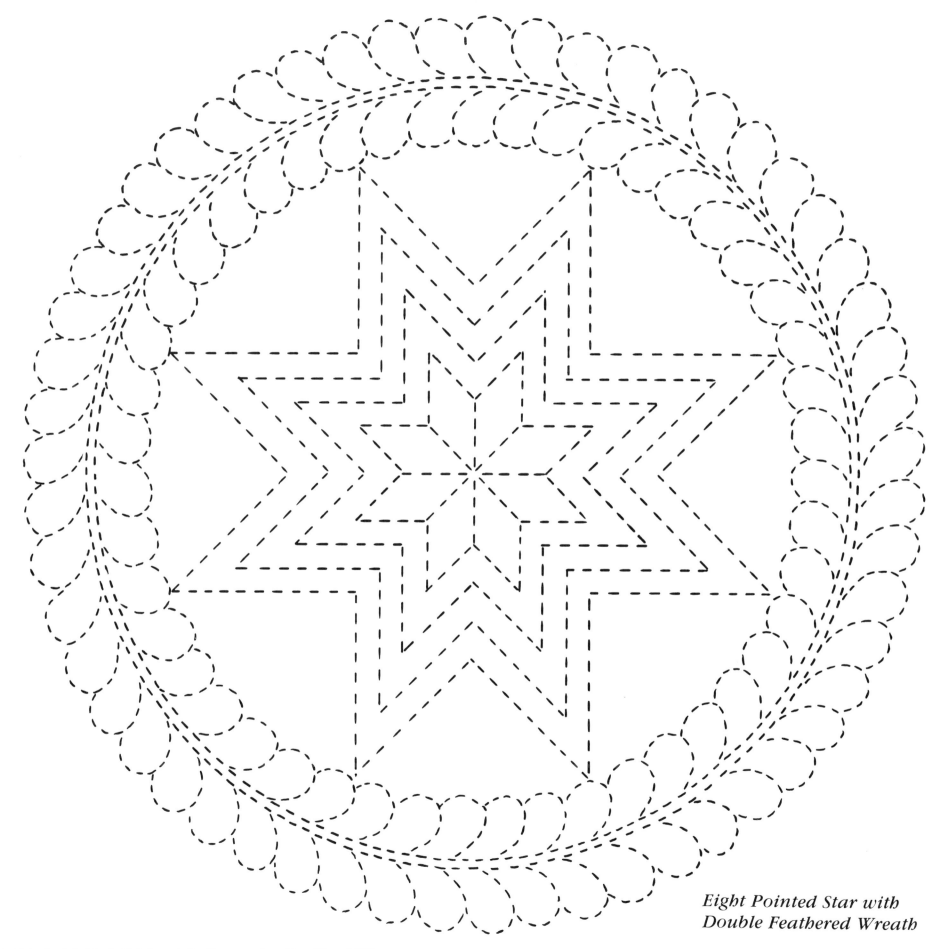

Eight Pointed Star with Double Feathered Wreath

As seen in *Lady's Circle Patchwork Quilts* magazine, Nov./Dec. 1989, Issue #66. Can be combined with the *Pumpkin Seed* design, page 14.

42

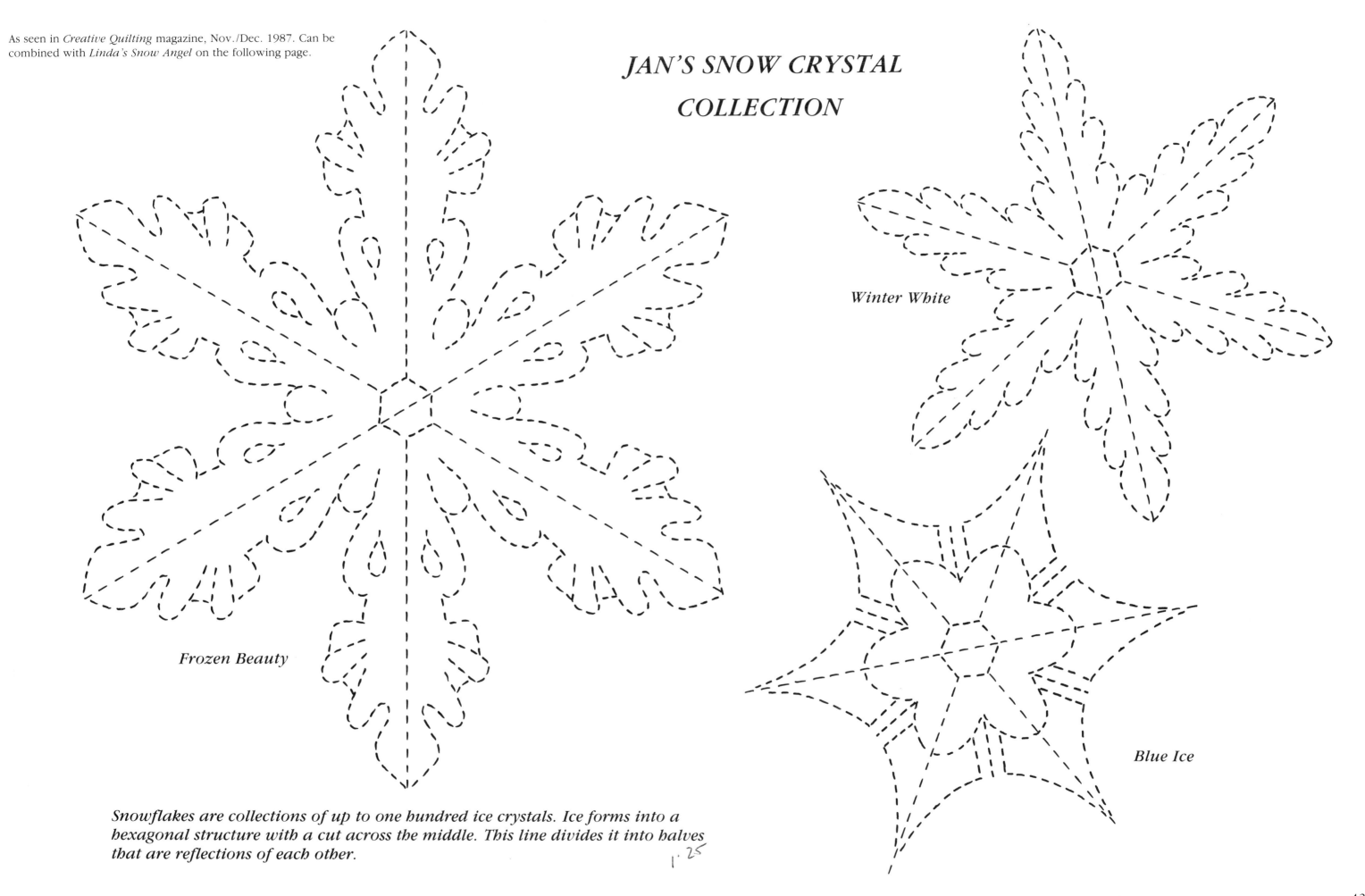

As seen in *Creative Quilting* magazine, Nov./Dec. 1987. Can be combined with *Linda's Snow Angel* on the following page.

JAN'S SNOW CRYSTAL COLLECTION

Winter White

Frozen Beauty

Blue Ice

Snowflakes are collections of up to one hundred ice crystals. Ice forms into a hexagonal structure with a cut across the middle. This line divides it into halves that are reflections of each other.

1·25

Linda's Snow Fairy

As seen in *Creative Quilting* magazine, Nov./Dec. 1989. Can be used with *Jan's Snow Crystal Collection* on the preceeding page.

Interlocking Scrolls

FRANCINE

To draft *Francine,* the *Interlocking Scrolls* version, first lock together two patterns then flip both to the next corner. Connect the design at the center with a small semi-circle and a curved line. Fold pattern in half diagonally and trace to opposite side. The final design can be made to appear elaborate or simple by adding flowing lines or eliminating curliques, as in the *Scroll Border* version below.

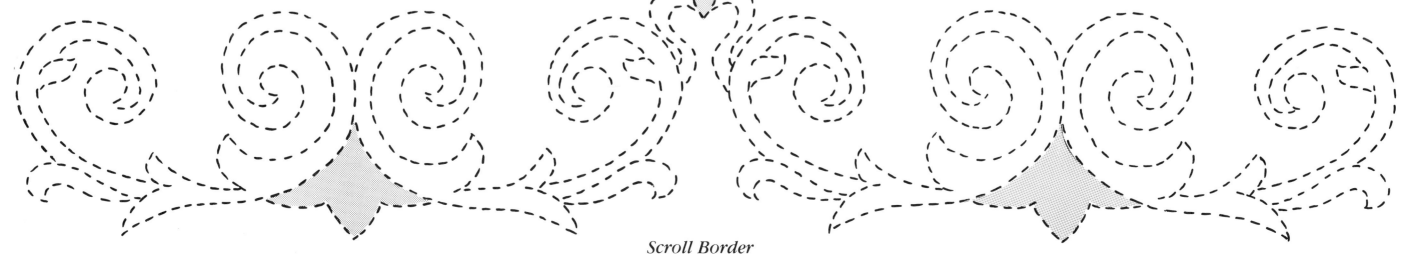

Scroll Border

DOUBLE WEDDING RING CEREMONY

Ring Bearer's Pillow Design

The perfect gift—

Picture the ring bearer walking down the aisle proudly carrying his small pillow. It is made in the *Double Wedding Ring* quilt pattern. It is pieced with colorful scraps from the Bridemaid's dresses and the white fabric of the Bridal gown.

This design of double rings tied with a bow is quilted in the middle. Sound nice? It is. I have made serveral Ring Bearer's Pillows as keepsake wedding gifts.

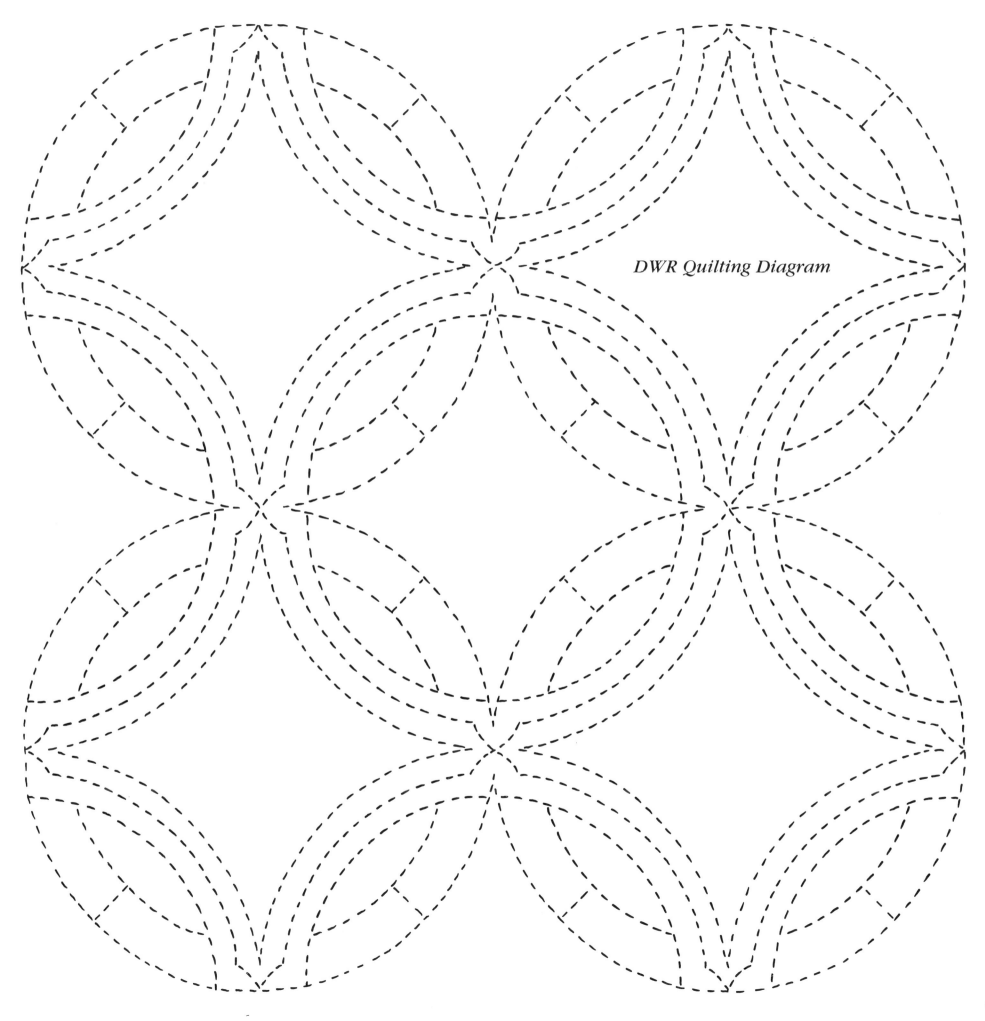

DWR Quilting Diagram

46

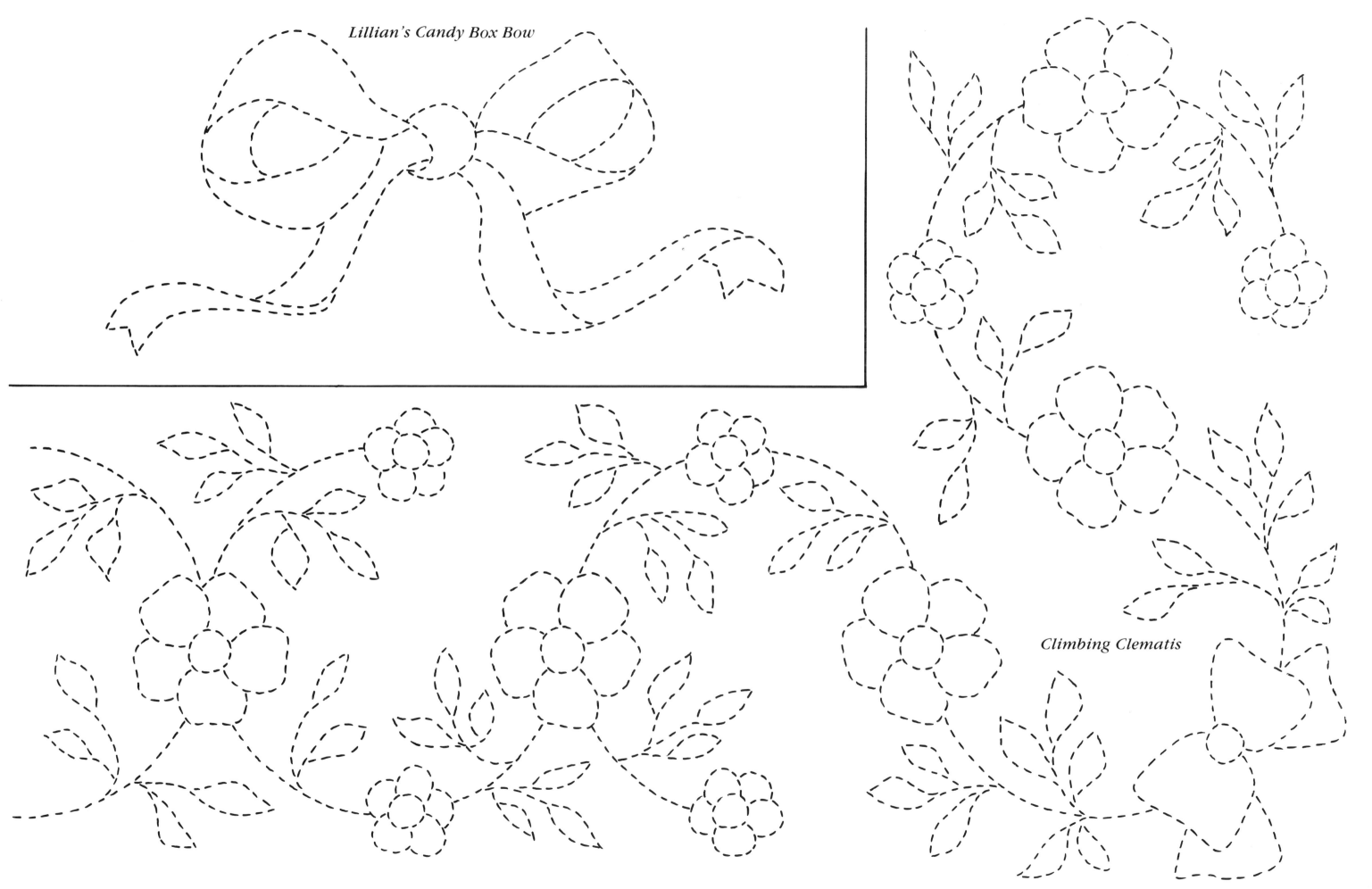

Lillian's Candy Box Bow

Climbing Clematis

47

A frame of bars, or uniform lines, is referred to as a grid. They are necessary for holding batting in place in bigger areas of background space. Detach these pages from the book. Match and join together with transparent tape to make larger repeats of the patterns. Grids are positioned under the fabric, after you finish sewing and pressing the quilt top. Copy straight lines with a ruler.

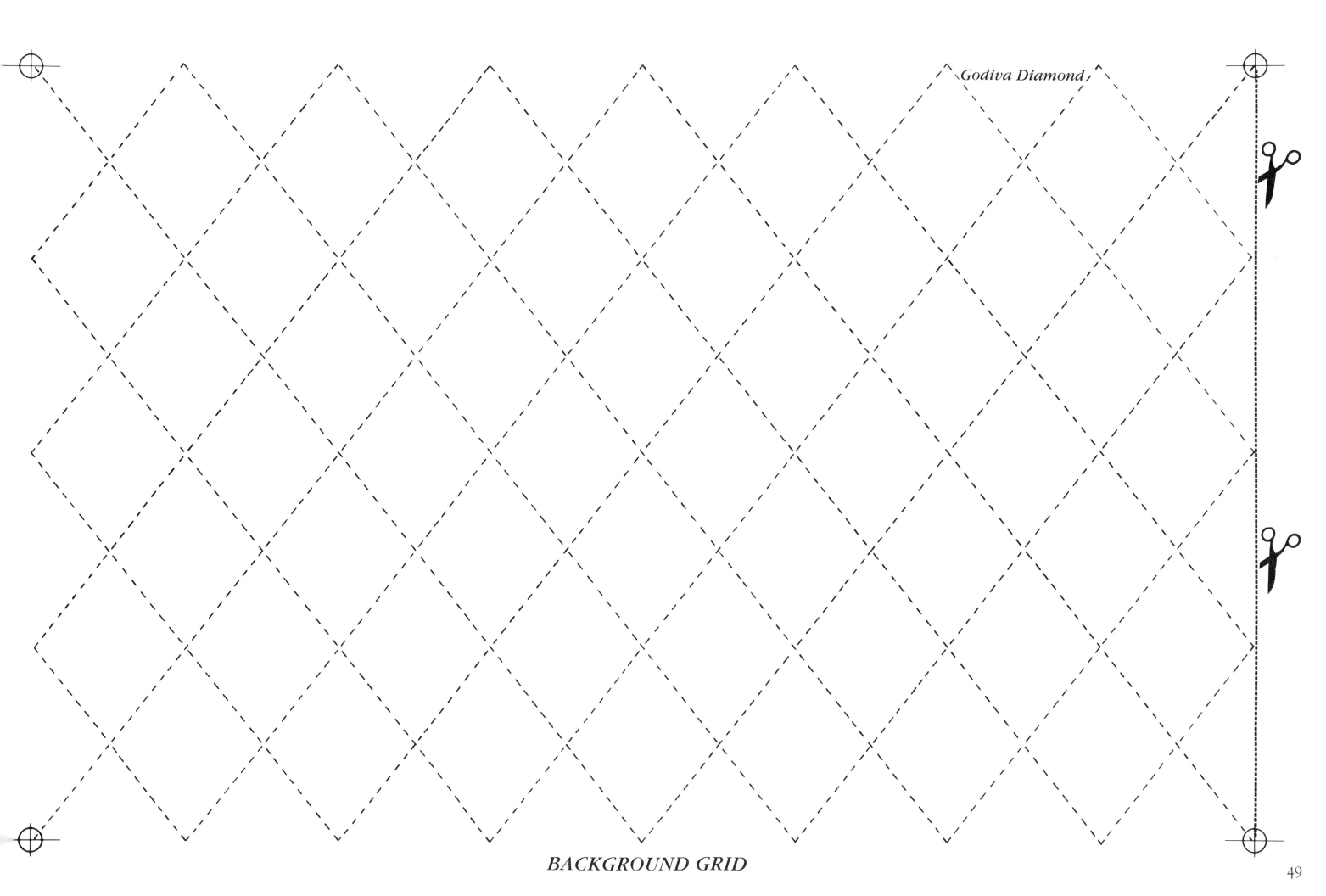

Godiva Diamond

BACKGROUND GRID

49

Godiva Diamond

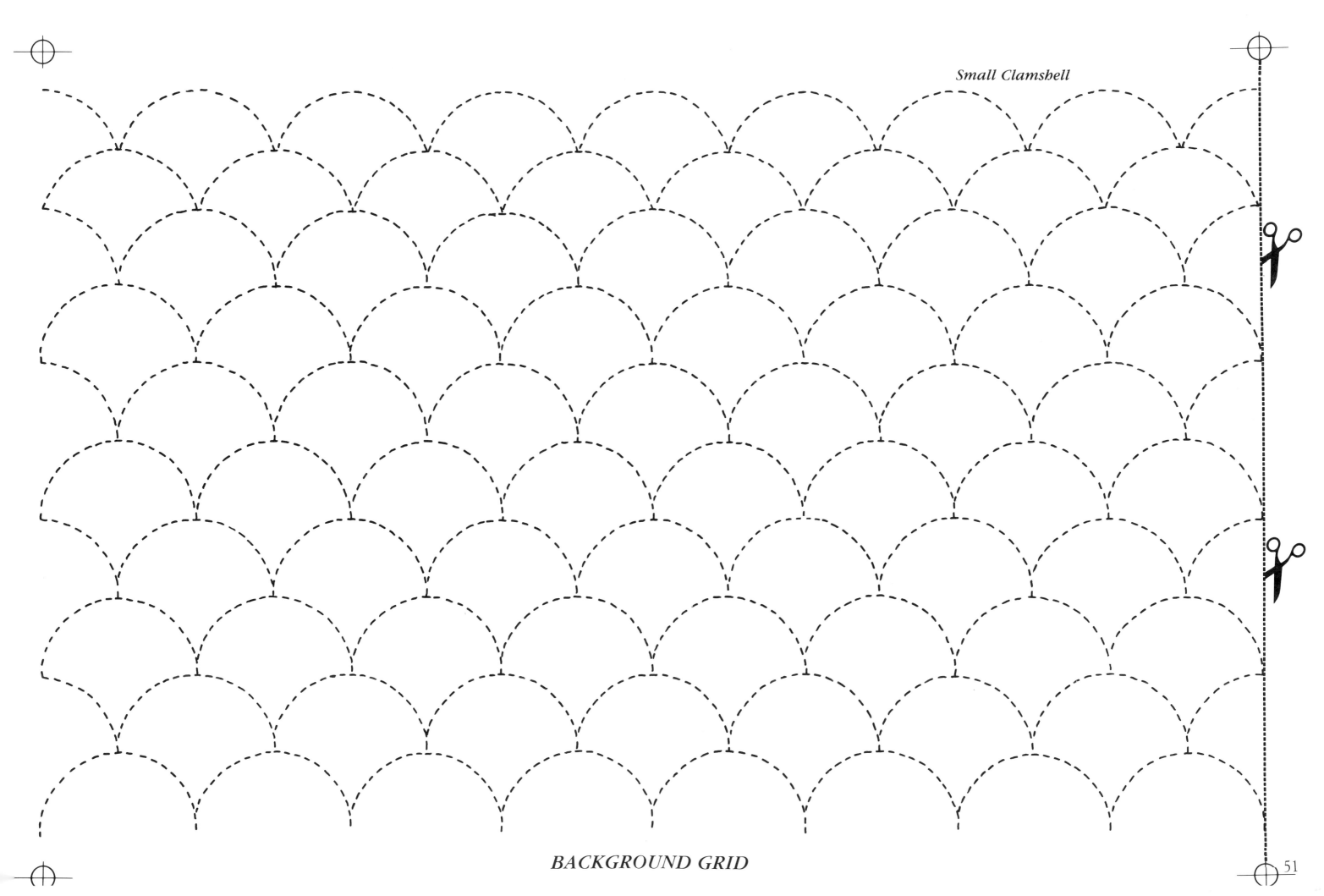

Small Clamshell

BACKGROUND GRID

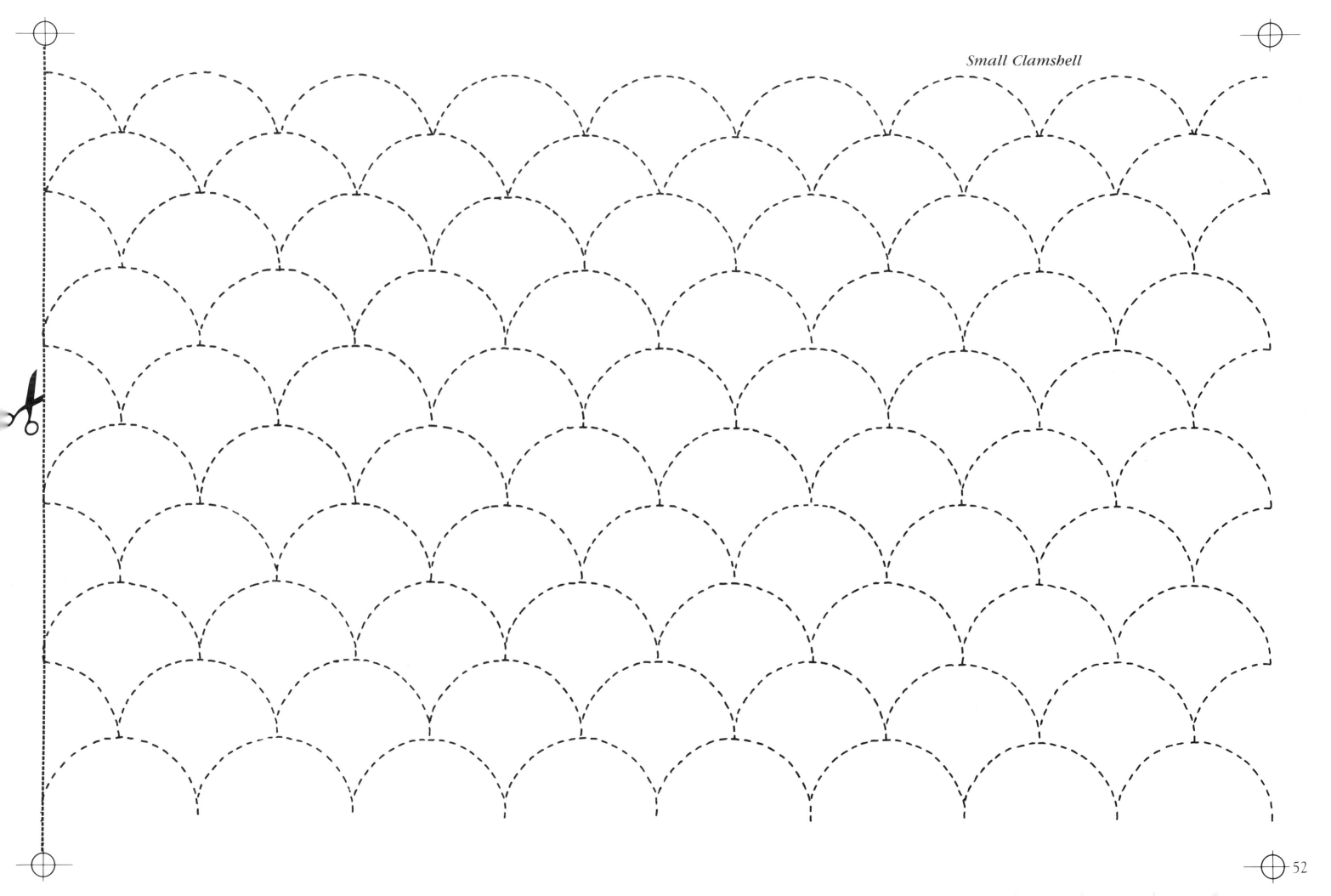

Small Clamshell

Large Clamshell

BACKGROUND GRID

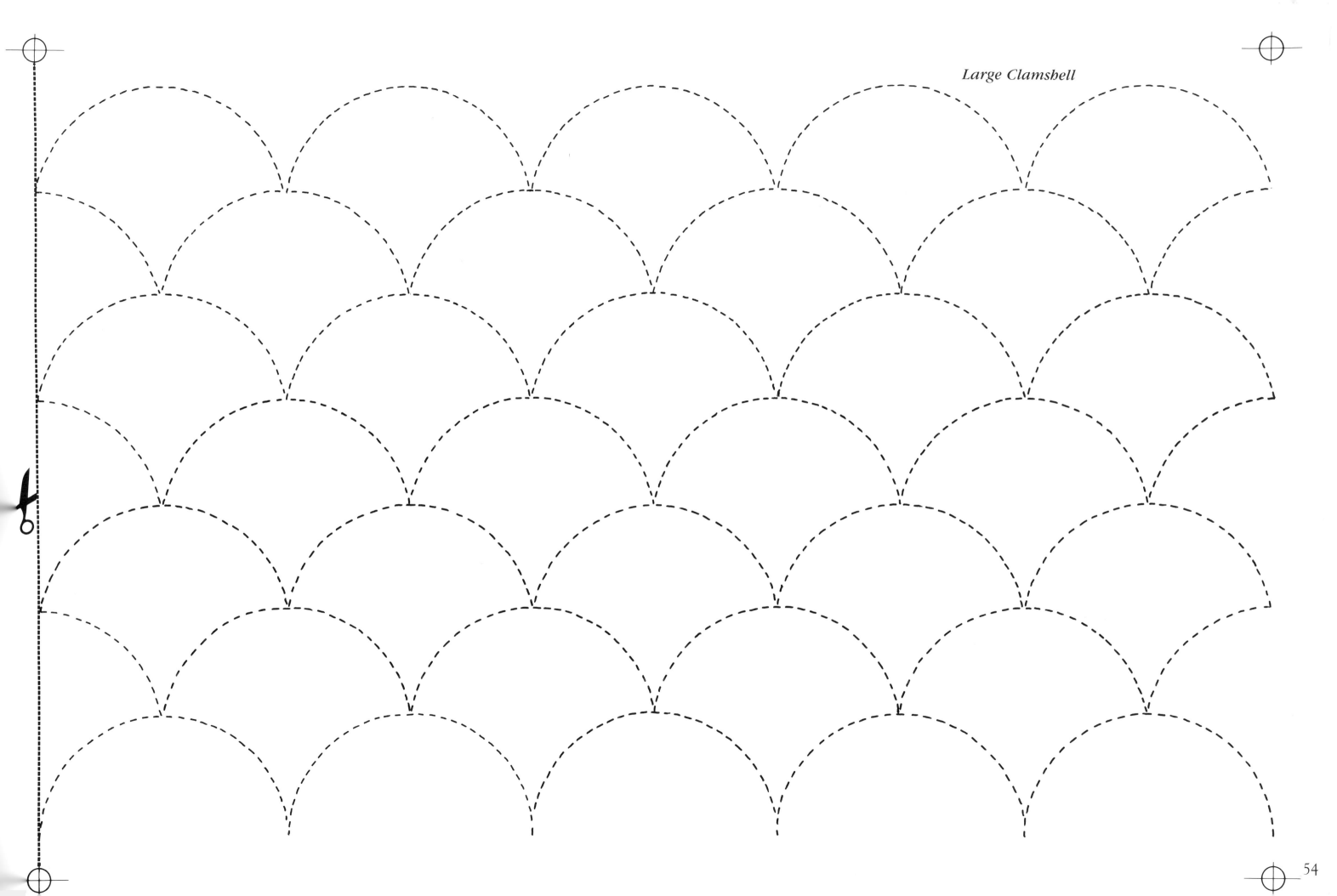

Large Clamshell